PRO FOOTBALL
TRIVIA

PRO FOOTBALL
TRIVIA

More Than 950 of the Most Challenging NFL Questions Ever!

BOB GILL

MASTERS PRESS

NTC/Contemporary Publishing Group

Library of Congress Cataloging-in-Publication Data

Gill, Bob.
    Pro football trivia : more than 950 of the most challenging NFL
questions ever / Bob Gill.
        p.   cm.
    Includes index.
    ISBN 1-57028-232-3
    1. Football—Miscellanea.   I. Title.
GV950.5.G55   1998
796.332—dc21   98-38538
                                              CIP

Cover design by Nick Panos
Cover illustrations by Dan Krovatin
Interior design by Kim Heusel
Interior illustrations copyright © 1997 The Learning Company, Inc., and its licensors

Published by Masters Press
A division of NTC/Contemporary Publishing Group, Inc.
4255 West Touhy Avenue, Lincolnwood (Chicago), Illinois 60712-1975 U.S.A.
Copyright © 1999 by Bob Gill
Printed in the United States of America
International Standard Book Number: 1-57028-232-3
                  04 QV 19 18 17 16 15 14 13 12 11 10 9 8 7

For my dad,
who enjoyed those baseball quiz books as much as I did

Contents

Preface .... *ix*

Game 1

1st Quarter
Milestones 1
2nd Quarter
Second Careers 5
3rd Quarter
Teams 8
4th Quarter
Nicknames 11

Game 2

1st Quarter
AFL *Pioneers* 13
2nd Quarter
Draft Day 17
3rd Quarter
All in the Family 21
4th Quarter
Moments to Remember 25

Game 3

1st Quarter
Notorious 29
2nd Quarter
Teammates 33
3rd Quarter
Spring Fever 37
4th Quarter
Point Men 41

Game 4

1st Quarter
Yesterday's Heroes 45
2nd Quarter
Men of Letters 49
3rd Quarter
Shooting Stars 52
4th Quarter
Black Pioneers 56

Game 5

1st Quarter
All in the Family 61
2nd Quarter
Stand-Ins 65
3rd Quarter
Milestones 70
4th Quarter
Gridiron Tragedy 74

Game 6

1st Quarter
Coaching Carousel 77
2nd Quarter
Notorious 81
3rd Quarter
Nicknames 85
4th Quarter
Odds and Ends 87

Game 7

1st Quarter
Teams 91
2nd Quarter
Minor Leagues and Others 95
3rd Quarter
Get Your Kicks 99
4th Quarter
Breaking In 103

Game 8

1st Quarter
World Football League 107
2nd Quarter
Notorious 112
3rd Quarter
North of the Border 116
4th Quarter
Time Line 120

Game 9

1st Quarter
Hall of Fame 123
2nd Quarter
Nicknames 127
3rd Quarter
Last Hurrahs 129
4th Quarter
Many Happy Returns 133

Game 10

1st Quarter
NFL Pioneers 137
2nd Quarter
Milestones 141
3rd Quarter
Second Careers 144
4th Quarter
Teammates 148

Game 11

1st Quarter
Notorious 151
2nd Quarter
Yesterday's Heroes 155
3rd Quarter
North of the Border 159
4th Quarter
Nicknames 164

Game 12

1st Quarter
Moments to Remember 167
2nd Quarter
All in the Family 171
3rd Quarter
Shooting Stars 175
4th Quarter
Men of Letters 179

Game 13

1st Quarter
Coaching Carousel 183
2nd Quarter
AFL Pioneers 187
3rd Quarter
Draft Day 191
4th Quarter
Before and After 195

Game 14

1st Quarter
Yesterday's Heroes 199
2nd Quarter
Gridiron Tragedy 203
3rd Quarter
Breaking In 206
4th Quarter
Teams 210

Game 15

1st Quarter
Minor Leagues and Others 213
2nd Quarter
Teammates 218
3rd Quarter
Notorious 222
4th Quarter
Milestones 225

Game 16

1st Quarter
All in the Family 229
2nd Quarter
Spring Fever 233
3rd Quarter
Nicknames 237
4th Quarter
Odds and Ends 239

Answers 243

Preface

About 20 years ago I bought a paperback book called *The Absolutely Most Challenging Baseball Quiz Book Ever*, by David Nemec. My dad and I spent a week or two working our way through it, and it lived up to its name. Unlike virtually every other book in its genre, this one didn't rely on a bunch of you-know-it-or-you-don't questions, like "Who was the first man to hit four home runs in one game?" Instead, it focused on short summaries of hundreds of players' careers in question form, and even the ones we couldn't get (i.e., most of them) were interesting. I learned a lot from that book, and I really enjoyed it.

Almost immediately it occurred to me that books of that sort could be written about other sports, too—football, for instance. I kept hoping somebody would write one, but nobody did. Then, in the early 1990s, while serving as occasional editor of *The Coffin Corner*, a publication of the Pro Football Researchers Association, I started to write my own football questions along the lines of Nemec's and use them to fill up the back pages. Eventually I got hooked on the concept and started writing many more than I could ever use—until now.

I don't expect anyone to get all the questions in this book; I figure a well-informed fan with a pretty good sense of the game's history should get about 50 percent, and real experts might do as well as 75 percent or thereabouts. But my goal is that no matter how many answers you know, you'll still learn some interesting tidbits about pro football history.

That means all of pro football's history, too, not just the NFL and maybe the AFL of the 1960s. There are plenty of questions about the modern game, of course, but you'll also find some about the Canadian Football League, the USFL of the 1980s, the World Football League of the 1970s, and even a few about leagues you may never have heard of—not to mention the NFL's formative years.

The book is divided into 16 "games," each consisting of four "quarters" with about 15 questions apiece—that is, about one question for each minute of the regular season. The questions are organized in categories, most of which should be self-explanatory.

But maybe I should explain my use of the term "all-pro," which you'll encounter often. If I say someone was a two-time all-pro, that means there were two seasons in which he was a first-team choice on a major all-pro (or all-AFC or all-NFC) team, such as the one chosen by the Associated Press or *Pro Football Weekly*—or, in the early years, the *Green Bay Press-Gazette*. Second-team choices don't count, nor do teams selected by individual reporters or broadcasters, except a couple from the very early years. So, don't ask how I could say so-and-so never made an all-pro team when you saw him on the "All-Madden" show two years in a row; it's not the same thing.

I also mention the Pro Bowl a lot, when I want to use a somewhat broader standard, since the teams named for this game include substitutes, the rough equivalent of second-team all-conference selections.

You may notice that the book is rather top-heavy with questions about backs and receivers. That's sort of unavoidable; it's simply a result of the fact that there are few statistics for defensive players and none at all for offensive linemen. Even in the case of an outstanding guard, for instance, once you've said he played in six Pro Bowls, you've pretty well exhausted the available information. And as you're probably aware, football history includes many great catches, long runs, and game-winning field goals, but very few famous blocks. So although I've tried to give the defense and the offensive line their due, they're somewhat under-represented here just as they are in television and newspaper reports every season.

Well, that wraps up the preliminaries. The teams are on the field; you've won the coin toss. Your chance to test your pro football knowledge begins with the opening kickoff. All you have to do is turn the page.

Game 1

1st Quarter

Milestones

He was the NFL's first 1,000-yard rusher, averaging an amazing 8.4 yards per carry in 1934. It was his rookie year, but though he played through 1940, a string of injuries limited this Tennessee All-American to only 976 more yards after his great debut.

A solid player for four years with the Giants, this back hit the heights in 1949. He rushed for 634 yards, caught 35 passes for 711 more, and led the NFL in scoring by virtue of his 17 touchdowns. On top of that, he had a pair of 200-yard receiving games, which may still be a record for a back. A year later he set a record with a 218-yard rushing effort, making him the only player to hit the 200-yard mark in each category; but after that he jumped to Canada, which is one reason he's largely forgotten today. Do you remember this versatile star?

The first man to amass 200 yards rushing in a game did it in 1933 for the Redskins, gaining 215 yards on 16 carries. Two things make this especially noteworthy: He did it against the Giants, a very strong team that won the Eastern Division that year; and it was 16 years until anybody else crossed the 200-yard barrier. Who was this Hall of Famer?

On November 8, 1970, his record-setting 63-yard field goal on the game's final play gave the Saints a 19–17 victory over the Lions. Even more amazing, he booted it with a right foot that had no toes.

In 1963 this end from Rice broke Don Hutson's career records for receptions and yardage, but it didn't get him into the Hall of Fame. He broke the records while wearing a Cowboys uniform, but most of his career was spent with Hutson's old team. One thing that hurt our man is that Raymond Berry broke his records soon afterward.

Only one man has ever gained 1,000 yards rushing and 1,000 yards receiving in the same season. He did it with the 49ers in 1985, catching a league-leading 92 passes in the process. Three years later he rushed for 1,502 yards and caught 76 passes. Can you name this Nebraska alumnus who finished his career with the Vikings in 1993?

The only other running back to gain 1,000 yards receiving did it the same year as the last man. Though he caught six fewer passes, his 1,027 yards set a record for running backs. He also rushed for 516 yards and returned kicks for nearly 1,000 more, giving him a combined total of 2,535 and another record. Who was this diminutive Chargers star?

Not to detract from the accomplishments of the last two men, but in 1958 and 1960 a Baltimore running back caught passes for 938 and 936 yards, respectively, in a 12-game season. (He had 846 yards in 1959.) If we use yards-per-game as the standard, obviously he's the greatest pass-catching back of all time. His efforts didn't go unnoticed, either; he was a consensus all-pro each year from 1958 through 1961. Who is this Hall of Famer?

 No one in the NFL has ever gained 300 yards passing and 100 yards rushing in the same game, but in 1950 a Hall of Fame quarterback missed doing so by a mere 3 yards when he passed for 298 yards (and four TDs) and ran for 99. Even more impressive is the fact that it came in the championship game. Who is this all-time great?

 In 1972 this Kansas alumnus gained 968 yards rushing for the Bears. What's so great about that? Well, he was a quarterback, and no other QB has ever matched that total. Unfortunately he completed only 38 percent of his passes that season, and the Bears finished 4–9–1.

 This quarterback from Georgia had such an original style that the writers of his time had to coin a new term for it: scrambling. By the time he hung up his cleats in 1978, he had rushed for 3,674 yards, more than any other quarterback. If you add the fact that he also retired as the career leader in passing yards and touchdowns, you'll probably conclude that we're talking about a Hall of Famer. And you'll be right.

 The career rushing record for QBs stood until 1992, when this man broke it in what was really only his seventh season (an injury sidelined him for all but a few plays in 1991). Two years earlier he made a run at the single-season rushing mark for QBs but fell just short with 942 yards. Since he also threw 30 touchdown passes that year, no one was complaining.

One of Vince Lombardi's key decisions as coach of the Packers was to turn this former Michigan star into the first true tight end. An outstanding blocker, he served as a "third tackle" but still had the ability to get open in the secondary. The move worked so well that he was an all-pro selection in 1961 and '62, and a major player on Lombardi's first two championship teams. Who is this pioneer?

 Who holds the record for most career receptions by a tight end? In 13 years with the Browns he caught 662 passes and reached his high point in 1983 and '84, with 89 each year.

Game 1

2nd Quarter

Second Careers

 This running back from Cornell didn't distinguish himself during a six-year NFL career, most of it spent with the Vikings. But he finished second in the Heisman Trophy voting in 1971, and after leaving football behind he made a name for himself as one of the stars of *Hill Street Blues*.

 After his rookie season with the Bears in 1929, this outstanding guard didn't play football for two years while he was in medical school. Returning in 1932, he was a key member of a Bears team that came within one quarter of winning three straight championships. An all-pro each year from 1933 through 1935, he moved to Detroit in 1936, then retired to continue his work as a doctor.

In an 18-year NFL coaching career, all with the same team, he did everything but win the Super Bowl. But in 1950, as a backup forward, he helped the Minneapolis Lakers win the NBA title.

 A supporting part on *Little House on the Prairie* gave this Hall of Fame defensive tackle his break as an actor, and before long he was playing the title role in *Father Murphy*.

 One of the top quarterbacks of the 1960s was also a talented golfer who found time to play in a number of tournaments on the PGA tour. That didn't stop him from playing 17 years in the NFL, all with the same team, and being chosen as the league's MVP in 1970.

 The only man enshrined in Canton and Cooperstown is this great lineman of the 1920s and '30s. Huge for his era at 6'5"and 250 pounds, he starred at tackle and end with four championship teams (one in New York, three in Green Bay). His size also lent an air of authority to his work as an umpire in baseball, which earned him a spot in that sport's Hall of Fame. Who was this mountain of a man?

 Another who enjoyed a long career as a baseball umpire was this Providence alumnus who broke into pro football with the Boston Shamrocks of the AFL in 1936 and led them to the championship. Two years later he caught a pass from Ed Danowski for the winning touchdown in the Giants' 23–17 victory over the Packers in the NFL title game. His first name was Albert, but everyone knew him by a variation of his middle name.

 The first choice in the 1967 draft, this defensive end from Michigan State starred with the Colts until a knee injury curtailed his effectiveness. After hanging up his cleats, he turned to acting, and though he'll never win any awards, he has achieved some success in movies such as *Police Academy* and its sequels. His parents named him Charles, but you'll know him by another name.

What coach, winner of three Super Bowls, left football behind to concentrate on his new role as the owner of a successful racing team on the NASCAR circuit?

 This defensive back, perhaps the finest of the '90s, has also spent a few summers as an outfielder for several major league teams. Though his baseball career hasn't matched his exploits on the football field, he had a couple of solid seasons.

 After an outstanding career as a defensive tackle, this former Lion scored a surprising success as a sitcom actor, though he was usually upstaged by the show's diminutive child star.

 Joining the Bengals in 1970, this All-American defensive tackle from Penn State was a perennial all-pro before retiring in his prime after the 1974 season to pursue a musical career. He went on to establish himself as a writer of hit country songs.

 The greatest player of pro football's early years spent six summers moonlighting as a major league outfielder. Altogether he hit only .252, but in his final season, playing for the New York Giants and the Boston Braves, he compiled a .327 average as a part-timer. Who was this all-time great?

 After seven fine years with the Raiders and the Chiefs in the early AFL, this defensive back launched a career as a star in action movies such as *Black Caesar* and *Hell Up in Harlem*. He also had a very short run as an announcer on *Monday Night Football*.

Game 1

3rd Quarter

Teams

Several NFL teams started out in different cities with different names. Give the current identity of the following four teams:

 Boston Braves

 Decatur Staleys

 Dallas Texans

 Portsmouth Spartans

In an 11-year period beginning in 1967, this franchise reached the AFL or AFC championship game nine times. Advancing to the Super Bowl only twice during this stretch, the team won one and lost one. What team are we talking about? And while we're at it, who was its coach for all but the first two years of this period?

In 1967 this team went 11–1–2, but that one loss, in the season's final game, kept it out of the playoffs under the system the NFL was using at the time. (It was the first time a tie-breaker was ever used to determine a division champion.) Do you remember which team may have been the best also-ran in football history?

In the days before there was a season-ending championship game, this team finished second in 1929 despite a terrific 13–1–1 record. Its only loss was a 20–6 setback at the hands of the undefeated Packers, who won their first title that year. Can you name this great runner-up that scored 312 points while allowing only 86?

Over an 18-year stretch beginning in 1966, this team won at least 10 games in all but three seasons, going 9–5 in 1967, 8–6 in 1974, and 6–3 in the strike year of 1982. In 12 of those seasons the team reached the NFL or NFC championship game, and in five trips to the Super Bowl it won twice. Can you name the team and its Hall of Fame coach?

In the 1960s the NFL held an annual game called the Playoff Bowl that matched the second-place teams in each conference. The first three games were all won by the same team, over three different opponents. What team was it?

This small-town team thought it had clinched the 1925 championship after beating the Cardinals in a key late-season game. In the glow of victory, it scheduled a game with a team of Notre

Dame all-stars for the following weekend. The NFL office disapproved and told the team to cancel the game or be kicked out of the league. The team played anyway (and won) and was immediately expelled from the NFL, making it ineligible for the championship the fans thought it had already won. Decades later, people in the town still claimed the NFL had stolen their championship. What team are we talking about?

 In 1972, a year after the death of owner Dan Reeves, the Rams were sold to a new man, who almost immediately swapped franchises with the owner of the Colts, then 3,000 miles away in Baltimore. The teams stayed put; only the two owners made a cross-country move. Who were they?

 The NFL added 10 teams when it merged with the AFL in 1970. Three other current NFL teams came from other leagues: two from the AAFC, and one from the AFL of 1936–37. Who are they?

 The NFL has outlasted or merged with several competing leagues, from Red Grange's AFL in 1926 to the USFL of 1983–85. Of more than 20 seasons when there were two major leagues, only once have both champions come from the same city. Can you name the year and the two winners?

 The first title game played at a neutral site came three decades before the Super Bowl was born. The game was moved because the owner of the home team was feuding with the fans and the local press. After losing the championship game, he moved the team to the city it still calls home. What team are we talking about?

Game 1

4th Quarter

Nicknames

The Brooklyn Dodgers spent 15 years in the NFL (1930–44; name changed to the Tigers in '44) without ever winning a division title. They came close twice, finishing second in 1940 and '41. Two of their best players were a Hall of Fame tailback who was the MVP in 1940 and a fullback who led the league in rushing in 1941. They were both named Clarence. But they went by much more suitable monikers. Who are we talking about?

From now on, I'll just give the nickname and you add the player's last name—and the first name too, if necessary:

2 Bam (either of two running backs)

3 Bambi

4 Big Daddy

5 Big Mo. And while we're at it, what about Little Mo?

6 Bones

7 Boomer

8 Broadway Joe

9 Bruiser

10 Bubby

11 Bucko

12 Bulldog

13 Bum

14 The Bus

15 Cannonball

Game 2

1st Quarter

AFL Pioneers

 The Dallas Texans used this rookie as a defensive back in the AFL's inaugural season, but the Raiders turned him into a running back when they picked him up a year later. He was one of the league's best from 1962 until he suffered a broken ankle late in the 1967 season. The league's leading rusher in 1963, he was also a terrific receiver out of the backfield. Do you remember him?

 Whether as a defensive tackle or a defensive end, this SMU alumnus was a standout for the Texans/Chiefs from 1961 through 1970. A six-time all-AFL performer, he never missed a game in his 10 seasons.

A 17th-round draft pick in 1962, this tackle was the backbone of the defense that led Buffalo to back-to-back championships in 1964 and '65. In a seven-year career, all with the Bills, he was a four-time all-AFL selection.

 This wide receiver from Stanford was an AFL original. In eight seasons, all with the same team, he caught 391 passes for 55 touchdowns and was a key player for two AFL championship squads, one in Dallas and one in Kansas City. Do you remember the Chiefs' leading receiver in Super Bowl I?

 In its early years the AFL was known for its wide-open passing game that led to high totals in yardage and interceptions. The Eastern Division in 1964 provides the classic illustration of this style. Buffalo split the quarterback job between two men who totaled 3,422 yards and 34 interceptions. The Patriots got 3,465 yards, 31 TDs, and 27 interceptions from their top QB. The Jets' starter didn't gain as much yardage but tossed 25 interceptions. And the top gun for the Oilers amassed 3,287 yards to go with 27 interceptions. Four of these QBs were all-AFL selections at least once; give yourself full credit if you know them, and take an extra pat on the back if you can name the Jets' starter.

 At 6'6" and 280 pounds, this product of Ohio State was one of the first gigantic offensive linemen. He joined the Dallas Texans in 1961 and stayed with them when they moved to Kansas City (and later to the NFL). A 10-time all-pro, he was a consensus all-AFL tackle in the league's last five years of existence.

 After short trials with the Eagles and in Canada, this wide receiver joined the New York Titans in the AFL's inaugural season. Later with the Raiders, he was one of the league's top deep threats from 1960 through 1966, leading twice in yardage and twice in TD receptions.

An all-AFL selection three years in a row, this tackle from Colgate was a mainstay in the offensive line for an Oilers team that reached the title game in each of the league's first three seasons. A bad back forced him out of football in 1963, and Houston didn't have another winning season until 1967. Do you remember him?

A teammate of the last man, this original Oiler never missed a game in a nine-year career. An all-league guard every year from 1962 through 1967, he played in four championship games with Houston. In a fitting end to a fine career, he played his final game in Super Bowl III, starting at guard for the Jets. Who is this standout from Kentucky?

Of all the veteran quarterbacks signed when the AFL was born, this Boston College standout may have been the most widely traveled. He started his pro career in 1950 as a member of the Erie Vets in the minor league AFL, which was in its final season. He spent a couple of years as a starter with the Hamilton Tiger-Cats and in 1954 threw the second-most touchdown passes of anyone in Canada. After that he played semipro ball off and on until the Patriots called in 1960. He and George Blanda were the only AFL passers to have more TDs than interceptions in each of the league's first two years, but after a poor year as a backup with the Titans in 1962 our man faded away again and was last seen with Hartford in the Continental League in 1966.

This Chargers halfback was one of the AFL's first stars, finishing among the rushing leaders five times in the league's first seven seasons, despite missing the entire 1962 season with a knee injury. After gaining a league-leading 1,121 yards in 1965, he faded quickly and finished with the Chiefs in 1969.

This linebacker was a consensus all-AFL choice for each of the league's first 5 seasons and played 13 seasons altogether, all with the Titans/Jets. He was one of the mainstays of the Jets defense that shut down the Colts in Super Bowl III.

This USC alumnus, a standout at tackle and guard, was probably the AFL's best offensive lineman. A consensus all-AFL choice for the first nine years of the league's existence, he was the second AFL player inducted into the Hall of Fame, a year after Lance Alworth, his teammate with the Chargers.

 This halfback was one of the AFL's finest all-around players in its early years, leading at various times in rushing, punt returns, and kickoff returns. Also an outstanding receiver out of the backfield, he did yeoman work for the Texans/Chiefs and the Broncos, and finished with the Jets in 1967.

Game 2

2nd
Quarter

Draft Day

The first player chosen in the 1975 draft, this quarterback struggled for a few seasons but made it big in 1980, throwing 31 touchdown passes and leading the Falcons to a 12–4 record. He threw 30 more a year later and was the NFL passing leader in 1983. Injuries caught up with him after that, and he was finished after the 1986 season, which he spent with the Rams. Who is this former California Golden Bear?

The Bears struck gold in the first round of the 1965 draft. Having stockpiled three No. 1 picks, they used two of them to select future Hall of Famers who are considered among the best ever at running back and linebacker, respectively, though in both cases their careers were shortened by knee injuries. Who are these two all-time greats?

A year earlier the Redskins had pulled off a similar draft-day coup. In the first round they chose a halfback from Arizona State who retired 13 years later as the career leader in receptions; in the second round they picked a defensive back from Iowa who now holds the career record for interceptions. Can you name this terrific twosome?

The Cardinals took this quarterback from Rice with the first pick in the 1958 draft, but he completed only one pass as a rookie, and that proved to be an omen for his entire career. He hung on for 12 years but never spent a whole season as a starter, though he did do some good work as a punter. His best years came with the Eagles in the '60s, and he returned to the Cardinals for his finale in 1969. Many fans probably thought he was known by a nickname, but actually he went by his real middle name. Who is he?

The Rams used the first choice in the 1963 NFL draft to grab this Heisman Trophy winner from Oregon State. But they spent the next three years trying to find out whether he was better at quarterback or halfback, before finally deciding he wasn't good enough at either position. He was last seen in 1967 with the Edmonton Eskimos of the CFL. Can you name him?

Besides being one of the top kick returners in the NFL today, this Florida State alumnus has an unusual distinction in that he had already played a year of pro football before being drafted by the Chiefs in 1995. He had spent the previous season playing with the Las Vegas Posse, part of the Canadian Football League's short experiment with teams based in the United States.

7. Just a few years ago this team used its first pick, the third overall, to take a star quarterback from Tennessee who eventually signed a multimillion-dollar contract. In the seventh and final round, the same team picked a Tulsa quarterback who signed for the league minimum. By the end of their second season, though, the obscure seventh-round pick was firmly ensconced as the team's starter. The Tennessee star found himself with a new team in 1997, where he threw for two touchdowns and 14 interceptions. Who are these two signal callers, and what team drafted them?

8. The Packers' first pick in the 1959 draft, this All-American quarterback from Iowa never played a down with Green Bay. His only taste of professional action came in 1961, when he completed 37 percent of his passes as a backup with the Dallas Texans. Can you name this QB who didn't make the grade as a pro?

9. When the Dolphins signed head coach Don Shula in 1970, the Colts protested that he was still under contract to them and charged Miami with tampering. Commissioner Pete Rozelle agreed and gave the Colts Miami's No. 1 pick in the following year's draft as compensation. When the time came, Baltimore picked an All-American from North Carolina who had led the nation in rushing. Used mainly as a short-yardage goal-line runner, he lasted 11 years in the NFL, all with the Colts.

10. Since the inception of the NFL draft in 1936, only one player without college experience has ever been chosen in the first round. And it didn't happen in the dim past—in fact, this defensive tackle was the Cardinals' top pick in 1991. They discovered him playing for the Bay State Titans of Lynn, Massachusetts, in the short-lived Minor League Football System.

In 1974 the Steelers may have had the most productive draft day ever. In the first five rounds they drafted two Hall of Famers—a center and a middle linebacker—plus two wide receivers who caught nearly 900 passes between them. It's probably no coincidence that Pittsburgh won its first Super Bowl that season. Can you identify the four draft picks that put the Steelers over the top?

 The first Heisman Trophy winner was also the first player chosen in the first NFL draft. He's famous enough on both counts that you shouldn't need any more clues to get him.

 Joe Montana was the last player taken in the third round of the 1979 draft, but three quarterbacks were chosen in the first round that year. One of them went on to be a star in his own right and was the MVP in Super Bowl XXI; one played regularly for his first two years with the Chiefs and finished with the Bears in 1986; and one, the No. 3 pick in the draft, played regularly with the Bengals in 1980 and had his only full season as a starter with Tampa Bay in 1983. At one time, though, they were all more highly regarded than Super Joe. Give yourself full credit if you can name two of them.

 The Colts used the first pick in the 1992 draft to grab this defensive end, a college star with the Washington Huskies. Plagued by injuries, he played only 18 games with them over the next three years; the high point came in his rookie year when he returned an interception 90 yards for a touchdown. He finally got in a couple of full seasons with Miami in 1995 and '96, but he was with another team in 1997, and for only three games at that. Who is he?

Game 2

3rd Quarter

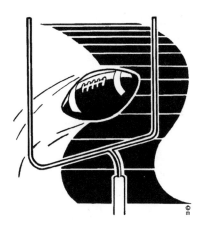

All in the Family

 These two brothers both broke into the NFL in 1993, because the elder had spent two years in Canada after leaving Notre Dame. The younger, a Syracuse alumnus, spent the first four years of his career with the Vikings; his brother spent the 1996 and '97 seasons with the Carolina Panthers. They're both wide receivers and kickoff returners, and I haven't mentioned their first names because they're so unusual that it would give them away. I will say, though, that the elder's nickname is Rocket.

 The highest-scoring brother act in NFL history, these two kickers from Penn State each topped 1,000 points. The elder played on two Super Bowl winners with the Raiders; the younger earned championship rings with the Steelers and Giants and is one of the few players to top 100 points in playoff games.

 Born 13 years apart, both of these brothers enjoyed successful NFL careers. The elder rushed for 5,453 yards with the Patriots from 1973 through 1982. His little brother, a quarterback, is less than 1,000 yards short of that rushing total and has also passed for more than 23,000 yards and 150 touchdowns.

 A defensive lineman for the 49ers in the early 1950s fathered two sons who enjoyed outstanding careers in the 1980s and '90s. One son, named after the old man, was a fine linebacker with the Browns; his kid brother has been a perennial all-pro while playing guard, center, and tackle for the Oilers. Who are they?

 In 1997 these brothers were teammates with the Redskins. The elder, Dan, who had been in the NFL since 1985, played center on special teams, where he snapped the ball to his kid brother, a punter. In a further display of family solidarity, Dan also served as the punter's agent. Can you name the younger brother, who made his second trip to the Pro Bowl when the season was over?

 At one time, these brothers were the most famous football siblings, because there were six of them: Al, Frank, Fred, John, Phil, and Ted. And in 1921 five of them played for the same team. (Al was the odd man out, since he was playing for Akron that year.) You need two things here: the family name, and the name of the team with which all but one of them played their whole careers. Hint: The team wasn't much in the NFL but had seen better days in the unofficial Ohio League in the mid-1910s.

 The elder of these two Alabama alumni had a Hall of Fame career as a guard with the Patriots from 1973 through 1985. His brother played on the offensive and defensive lines for six years with the Buccaneers and six more with the Raiders. Not too much information here because of the Hall of Fame clue.

 In January 1973 dad was the quarterback who led the Dolphins to victory in Super Bowl VII; 25 years later, his son threw three TD passes to lead Michigan to victory in the Rose Bowl. If you need a hint, the father is in the Hall of Fame.

 In the 1980s four members of this family played in the NFL. The best of the bunch was Joey, several times an all-pro defensive back with the Vikings. Two of the others, Ross and Jim, were teammates with the Bengals in 1979 and '80. The fourth, Keith, played with four teams in a five-year career. What's their family name?

 In 1964 the Bills' quarterback threw 269 passes for 2,285 yards and 13 touchdowns. Twenty years later his son, playing with the Rams, threw 284 passes for 2,021 yards and 13 touchdowns. Can you name them?

 These brothers both played for teams in the NFC West in 1997. Michael, an Arizona product, led the NFL in kickoff returns in 1996 and '97; Mario, from Arizona State, rushed for 951 yards with the Saints in 1995. What's their last name?

 These two brothers were among the better linemen of the 1920s and '30s, and both started their pro careers with the Kansas City Cowboys and wound up with the Giants. The elder became one of the NFL's great coaches, reaching the championship game eight times and winning twice; his kid brother won three titles in the minor league American Association.

 Dick, the elder, was an outstanding safety with the Dolphins from 1968 through 1974, but he missed the 1975 season with a knee injury and wasn't the same after that. His kid brother

Bobby was a versatile runner and receiver with the Broncos from 1970 through 1973, but missed the 1974 season with a broken ankle and played only six games in 1975, his last season. With the added information that they both played college ball at Colorado, can you supply their last name?

 From 1981 through 1986 the Dolphins' defensive backfield included this pair of brothers. The younger played his whole nine-year career with Miami; the elder made stops in Cincinnati, Seattle, and Baltimore before teaming up with his sibling.

Game 2

4th Quarter

Moments to Remember

 With 44 seconds remaining in a 1975 playoff game, Roger Staubach connected on a 50-yard touchdown pass that gave the Cowboys a 17–14 victory over the Vikings. It came to be known as the "Hail Mary" play, but the Vikings thought it was less the result of divine intervention than a case of offensive interference by the Cowboys receiver, who had shoved cornerback Nate Wright before catching the pass. Who was the Dallas star who may have benefited from an official's noncall?

 His 43-yard touchdown run on a fourth-and-one play with just over 10 minutes remaining gave the Redskins a lead they never relinquished in Super Bowl XVII.

Two Hall of Fame quarterbacks put on an amazing show in a celebrated 44–34 shootout early in the 1972 season, setting a record for combined passing yards in a single game. The winning QB passed for 496 yards and six touchdowns; his counterpart threw for 376 yards and two scores. For the former, this was the best game of his last all-pro season; for the latter, it was the last outstanding game of his career. Who are these two superstars?

The 1958 championship game ended in a 23–17 victory for the Colts when this fullback scored from a yard out to end the first overtime game in NFL history.

Pro football's second overtime contest occurred in the 1962 AFL championship game, which ran into an unprecedented sixth period before the Dallas Texans won it on a 25-yard field goal by what rookie kicker from Alabama?

The 49ers earned their first trip to the Super Bowl by beating the Cowboys 28–27 in the NFC championship game in January 1982. What star receiver made a leaping catch of a pass from Joe Montana late in the fourth quarter for the winning score?

What former Maryland star caught three touchdown passes from Frank Ryan as the Browns upset the Colts 27–0 in the 1964 NFL championship game? It was his big moment in the spotlight, but in a 10-year career he also led the league with 13 TD receptions in 1963 and a 46.7-yard punting average in 1965.

The Dolphins' bid for a third straight championship was snuffed out in the first round of the 1974 playoffs when the Raiders scored in the game's final minute for an electrifying 28–26 victory. With a tackler clinging to his ankle, quarterback Ken Stabler tossed a dying quail into the end zone, and do you remember the running back who snatched the ball away from the Miami defenders?

 In a playoff game on Christmas Day, 1971, the Dolphins outlasted the Chiefs in a wild battle that required two overtime periods. But the day's real hero played for the losing team. He carried 17 times for 85 yards and a touchdown, caught eight passes for 110 yards and another score, and returned three kickoffs for 154 yards. He also had a 1-yard punt return, giving him a total of 350 all-purpose yards. Who was this Kansas City workhorse?

 The Cardinals won the 1947 NFL championship game when two star halfbacks each turned in a pair of long scoring runs. One of them scored on a pair of 70-yard runs from scrimmage; the other scored on a 44-yard run and a 75-yard punt return. It was just enough for a 28–21 victory, and the Cardinals haven't won a playoff game since. Who were these two breakaway backs?

 What rookie defensive back picked off a record four passes to lead the Oilers to a 17–14 win over the Chargers in a 1979 playoff game? When he wasn't bedeviling Dan Fouts, he also blocked an attempted field goal and returned it 57 yards to set up a Houston score.

 Playing on a mud-covered field a day after torrential rains hit Los Angeles, this great running back carried 31 times for 196 yards as his team beat the Rams in the 1949 championship game. In the process he set a playoff rushing record that stood for decades. You shouldn't need the team to get this one.

 Trailing the 49ers 27–7 early in the third quarter of a playoff for the Western Division title in 1957, the Lions rallied for a stunning 31–27 victory and earned a trip to the championship game. The comeback was spurred by a reserve running back who scored the first touchdown on a short run, then broke away minutes later on a 58-yard scoring play. He finished with 86 yards rushing in the game, which was more than the total he'd gained in his two seasons with the Lions. Sent to Pittsburgh a year later, he gave the Steelers three fine seasons before he started to slip. Who is he?

In the AFC championship game between Houston and Pittsburgh after the 1979 season, officials disallowed an Oilers touchdown that would have tied the game in the third quarter, ruling that the receiver didn't get both feet in bounds. The Steelers hung on for the victory, earning their fourth trip to the Super Bowl, but the call was so hotly disputed that it spawned the first serious talk about using instant replays to help officials. Do you remember the Oilers' quarterback and receiver who hooked up on this controversial play?

This 49ers running back scored a playoff–record five touchdowns, all by rushing, in a 44–3 rout of the Giants in January 1994. A Notre Dame product, he signed with the Seahawks after the 1997 season. Who is he?

Tied 10–10 with two minutes to go against the Browns in the final game of the 1958 regular season, the Giants won on a 49-yard field goal by a kicker who was playing his first season in New York after several years with the Cardinals. The victory in that game forced a playoff with those same Browns a week later, which the Giants also won, to set up the famous sudden-death championship game with the Colts. But it wouldn't have happened without that game-winning kick, which was made in a snowstorm. Can you name the kicker, who later became a highly respected TV announcer?

Game 3

1st Quarter

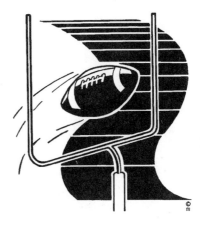

Notorious

1. By the late 1970s, some teams had started to have their quarterbacks kneel down to kill the clock at the end of games. But it didn't become a universal practice until November 19, 1978, when the Giants botched a handoff on what would have been the game's final play and saw a 17–12 victory turned into a 19–17 loss when Philadelphia cornerback Herman Edwards grabbed the loose ball and ran it back for a touchdown. Do you remember the Giants' quarterback and running back whose foul-up made the kneel-down de rigueur in the NFL? The running back's earlier exploits with another team earned him a spot in the Hall of Fame, but the QB might be tough.

2. The AFL scored its first coup when this Heisman Trophy winner signed with the Oilers in 1960. He led the AFL in rushing in 1961 and later served the Raiders well as a tight end. More than a decade after his playing career ended, he was back in the news when he pleaded guilty for his role in a million-dollar counterfeiting operation.

3. Who was the paroled convict from Sing Sing Prison who made headlines in 1935 when he signed with the Eagles? His prowess with the prison team had made him a national story, but though his presence gave attendance a shot in the arm, he showed little in the NFL and was released after three games.

4. In the opening minutes of a 1986 playoff game against the Giants, a 49ers receiver broke into the clear and was cruising in for an easy touchdown when he simply dropped the ball, couldn't manage to pick it up, and finally kicked it through the end zone for a touchback. The Giants went on to win 49–3. Who was the slippery-fingered 49er who set the tone for this annihilation?

5. Victimized by 34 sacks in 1997, this certain Hall of Famer known for his fourth-quarter comebacks has now been sacked more than any other quarterback in NFL history—498 times, to be exact.

6. Until the last man passed him, another contemporary quarterback owned the dubious distinction of being sacked the most times, with 492. (Though active in 1997, he threw only two passes and avoided adding to his total.) He's also second in another negative category, having fumbled 150 times. Despite that, he still managed to pass for 261 touchdowns and almost 38,000 yards. He played for a different team in each of the last five seasons but had his best years with his first team, for which he played from 1980 through 1991. Who is this three-time Pro Bowler?

This Raiders defensive back sued Chuck Noll in 1977 after the Steelers' coach referred to him as part of a "criminal element" in the NFL. After seeing film of him in action, the jury ruled in Noll's favor.

 The Colts found Johnny Unitas playing for a semipro team called the Bluefield Rams after he had been cut in training camp by the team that selected him in the ninth round of the 1955 draft. What was the team that had Unitas and let him go?

 The first pick in the 1990 draft, this quarterback finally showed signs of living up to his potential in 1995 with the Falcons, throwing for 4,143 yards. But he was summarily dropped for insubordination early in the next season after a much-replayed sideline tantrum directed at his coach. Who are we talking about? And for extra credit, what team picked him up in 1997?

 Before Super Bowl XIII, a Dallas linebacker made headlines when he claimed that the opposing quarterback was so dumb that he "couldn't spell cat if you spotted him the C and the A." The quarterback had the last laugh, passing for 318 yards and winning the game's MVP Award while leading his team to a victory over the Cowboys. Can you name him, and his Dallas detractor?

 In a 1982 contest played in a snowstorm in New England, the Patriots were lining up to try a 33-yard field goal in the fourth quarter of a scoreless game. With snow piled up on the turf, the kick was far from a sure thing. But during a time-out a snowplow driver slipped onto the field and cleared a space for the ball to be spotted, and the ensuing kick gave the Patriots a 3–0 win. Who was the kicker who made the controversial field goal? And what team did he beat? Hint: The kicker had led the AFC in scoring in 1979 and '80; the losing team wound up the season in the Super Bowl.

When the Chargers' starting quarterback was injured early in the 1962 season, the team wanted to put him on injured reserve. That meant putting him on waivers first, though—and at that point he was claimed by Buffalo for a mere $100. The Bills really rubbed it in when they beat the Chargers in the 1964 and '65 AFL championship games with their $100 QB at the helm. Who was the quarterback in question? And who was the Chargers' Hall of Fame coach who gambled on the waiver wire and lost?

 At a banquet early in 1985, a somewhat inebriated Redskins running back made headlines when he repeatedly advised Supreme Court Justice Sandra Day O'Connor to "Loosen up, Sandy baby; you're too tight." Who was this star who didn't know when to say when?

 One contender for the title of dullest postseason game ever was an NFC divisional playoff game in 1970 that ended with the highly unusual score of 5–0. The winning team's quarterback completed just 4 of 18 passes for 38 yards. What teams took part in this display of offensive firepower?

 What celebrated special teams player, a seven-time Pro Bowler, ended his 13-year career on an embarrassing note when he was ejected in the first quarter of the 1997 finale for arguing a call with an official? (Replays, incidentally, backed the official.)

Game 3

2nd Quarter

Teammates

Besides going undefeated, the 1972 Dolphins were the first team in NFL history to have two 1,000-yard rushers . . . maybe. Sure, Larry Csonka gained 1,117 yards; but the other man finished the season with 991. Then, a couple of days later, a zealous statistician discovered that the No. 2 man had been mistakenly credited with a 9-yard loss, which meant he really gained—surprise!—1,000 yards on the nose. What speedy halfback was the beneficiary of this recount?

One year later, a pair of Bengals fell 15 yards short of becoming the second pair of 1,000-yard rushers. They finished with 997 and 988, respectively. Can you name Cincinnati's dynamic duo?

What two backs were the second pair of teammates to reach the 1,000-yard mark? They did it in 1976, but their team failed in its bid for a third straight championship.

The advent of the 16-game schedule in 1978 could have brought more 1,000-yard tandems, but rule changes that increased the emphasis on the passing game offset the effect of an extra two games, as did most teams' increasing reliance on a single star running back. Still, in 1978 the Bears almost joined the exclusive club. Walter Payton, of course, was one of the backs; he led the NFC with 1,359 yards. Who was his backfield mate who fell just short with 992?

In 1985, unsure of rookie QB Bernie Kosar, the Browns relied on their ground game, and both starting backs finished with more than 1,000 yards—the third and last pair to do so. It wasn't easy, because one of them was still six yards short when the gun sounded to end the final game. But an offside penalty on Jets lineman Joe Klecko gave Cleveland a final offensive play, and our man picked up enough yards to finish with 1,002. Can you name him and his backfield mate?

Fans who remember the AFL's reputation as a pass-happy league probably won't be surprised to hear that the first team to have two receivers with more than 1,000 yards apiece was an AFL team in 1960, its inaugural season. If I tell you the team was the Titans, can you name the two receivers who amassed 2,432 yards and 20 touchdowns? One of them is in the Hall of Fame, and I'll add that they duplicated the feat in 1962.

Two Oilers receivers topped 1,000 yards in 1961, and in fact they surpassed the accomplishment of the Titans' duo. One of them gained a record 1,746 yards; the other hauled in 17 touchdown passes. Who were these Houston hotshots?

In 1962 and '63 the Cardinals just missed becoming the first NFL team with two 1,000-yard receivers. One of their wideouts topped 1,000 yards in each of those seasons, and the other came close, with 954 and 967, respectively. Each of them had one season as a consensus all-pro, and the second man led the NFL in receptions in 1963. Who are they?

 A pair of Cowboys receivers came even closer to having dual 1,000-yard seasons in 1967; the odd thing is that they both fell short of the magic number. One, known as "the world's fastest human," gained 998 yards; the other, playing his first season in Dallas after two seasons as a special-teamer with the Vikings, gained 996. Can you name them?

The NFL finally produced its first team with a pair of 1,000-yard receivers in 1979—and as it happened, three teams turned the trick. I'll give the teams, and you name the prolific pass catchers for each:

 Chargers

 Patriots

 Cowboys

 Just a year later, one of those three teams became the first to have three receivers with 1,000 yards or more—in this case, quite a bit more, as they combined for 3,762 yards. Can you name the team and each member of its terrific trio?

The next team to have a 1,000-yard trio did it in 1989. If I tell you Mark Rypien was the chief beneficiary of their efforts, can you tell me the team and the three receiving standouts?

Twenty-two years earlier the Redskins became the first team to have three players who caught at least 60 passes in the same season. Two of them are in the Hall of Fame; the other retired with the record for most touchdown receptions by a tight end.

Game 3

3rd Quarter

Spring Fever

 1. In the three years of its existence, the United States Football League managed to sign each reigning Heisman Trophy winner—two running backs and a quarterback. Can you name them?

 2. The Philadelphia Stars lost the USFL's first championship game by two points, then won the next two titles—the last of them representing a new home city, Baltimore. That performance earned their head coach a job as the head man in New Orleans, where he turned the perennially moribund Saints into a consistent playoff team for a half dozen seasons and was the NFL's Coach of the Year in 1987. Who is he?

3. The Stars' quarterback throughout their existence had spent a couple of years as a third-stringer with Tampa Bay, throwing a total of five passes. Three outstanding seasons in the USFL earned him a shot with the Packers in 1986, but he threw only 32 passes and dropped from sight after that. Who is this former Penn State star?

4. Actually, the Stars' best offensive player was a running back from North Carolina who was an all-USFL choice in 1983 and '84, and the Player of the Year in 1983. An outstanding runner and receiver, he later had three pretty good seasons with the Redskins until a succession of injuries finally finished him.

5. The USFL's first champs, the Michigan Panthers, were led on offense by a pair of rookies at quarterback and wide receiver who later enjoyed lengthy careers in the NFL. The receiver played nine years with the Vikings and had three 1,000-yard seasons. The quarterback played seven seasons with the Saints, leading them to their first playoff appearance, and had a couple of fine seasons with the Falcons. Do you remember the Panthers' dynamic duo?

6. An all-USFL selection in 1984 and '85, this offensive tackle has been a seven-time all-pro in the NFL with the Vikings and the Broncos. He retired in 1997 but was lured back during the season to shore up an offensive line that may have been the key to Denver's upset victory in the Super Bowl.

7. Another tackle who got his start in the USFL was this UCLA alumnus who was an all-league selection three years in a row with the Philadelphia/Baltimore Stars and went on to play 11 years in the NFL with five different teams. He spent the first five of those seasons with the Chiefs and was last seen with the Oilers in 1996.

The second-leading passer in the USFL's first season was a 29-year-old quarterback the Oakland Invaders had discovered playing with the Twin Cities Cougars of the semipro California Football League. He lost his starting job after a disappointing 1984 season and spent the USFL's final year as the backup QB for an Oakland team that made it all the way to the championship game. After that he drifted back into obscurity. Do you remember him?

 In 1984 and '85 combined, this back with the Tampa Bay Bandits rushed for 2,215 yards and caught 138 passes. He wasn't quite as good in the NFL, but he had a couple of good years with the Chargers, catching 80 passes in 1986 and rushing for 1,119 yards in 1988. Who was this former Arkansas star?

 Breaking in with the Chicago Blitz in 1983, this defensive back from Louisville was a three-time all-NFL choice with the Browns a few years later. Can you name him?

 The presence of this coach, owner of a .712 winning percentage in the NFL, made the Chicago Blitz the early favorites to win the first USFL championship. But though his teams did well, they suffered from a common USFL malady: an inability to beat the Stars in the playoffs. The Stars came back from a three-touchdown deficit to beat the Blitz in overtime in a 1983 division playoff; in 1984 they beat the Arizona Wranglers (now featuring the Chicago players from '83, plus their famous coach) in the championship game, which turned out to be our man's last appearance as a professional football head coach. Who was he?

 An all-USFL selection in each year of its existence, and the punting leader in 1985 with a 44.3-yard average, this Oakland Invaders star got only a one-year trial in the NFL, with the Raiders in 1987. He averaged 40.7 yards per kick and was sent packing after that. USFL experts will know him, but others might just scratch their heads.

The other standout punter who made his debut in the USFL has had far more success in the years since. After three seasons with the Stars, in one of which he was a consensus all-USFL choice, he joined the Giants in 1985 and was still around in 1997, when he averaged 42.1 yards per kick for Tampa Bay. His NFL career average is better than 43 yards, but in the USFL it was only 41.6. Who is this three-time all-pro?

 One of the game's greatest defensive ends, this sure Hall of Famer from Tennessee broke into the professional ranks in 1984 with the Memphis Showboats. He was an all-league selection in his second year, an accomplishment he repeated with great regularity in the NFL.

 The hapless Washington Federals had few strengths in 1983, but one of them was a back from SMU who rushed for 823 yards and caught 40 passes. An injury sidelined him for most of the 1984 season, and that fall he jumped to the NFL with the Patriots. There he showed what he could do with a real team, rushing for 1,227 yards in New England's Super Bowl season of 1985 before injuries caught up with him again. He hung on through 1988 but rarely suited up after 1986. Do you remember this college running mate of Eric Dickerson?

Game 3

4th Quarter

Point Men

In a six-year career this versatile Lions halfback led the NFL in scoring twice. He also finished third twice and second another year. A four-time all-pro, he was only 28 when he called it quits. Who is this former Heisman Trophy winner?

The first player to score 20 touchdowns in a season did it in 1964 for the Colts, bouncing back from an injury-plagued 1963 to lead the league in scoring and add a fifth all-pro season to his Hall of Fame portfolio. He totaled 113 touchdowns in his illustrious career. Who is this former Penn State star?

One year after the last man reached the 20-touchdown mark, two more all-time greats pushed the envelope a little further. One, playing his final season, scored 21 TDs; the other, a rookie, tallied 22 and led the NFL in scoring. Can you name them?

Ten years later, a future Hall of Famer with Buffalo set a new mark with 23 touchdowns, while a third-year Vikings star reached the end zone 22 times, matching the previous record. Who are these touchdown twins?

All of the previous touchdown record-holders were backs who scored via rushing and receiving, but the man who set a new mark of 24 TDs in 1983 got them all on the ground. Who is this burly Redskin?

Four years later a 49ers receiver made a run at the record but finished with "only" 23. He deserves special mention, though, for two reasons: first, this was the strike year that gave us "re-placement games," and he did all of his damage in what was really only a 12-game season; second, he caught 22 touchdown passes, 4 more than anyone else has ever caught.

The current touchdown record was set in 1995 by a running back who scored all of his 25 on the ground. Since he had tal-lied 22 a year earlier (21 by rushing), that gave him a two-year total of 47, another record.

From 1951 through 1953 this 49ers star caught 157 passes, scored 298 points, and played in three straight Pro Bowls. The NFL's scoring leader in 1952 and '53, he never matched those seasons but hung around through 1958 and scored a total of 644 points. Who is this Minnesota alumnus?

The only pure kicker to be chosen as MVP, this Redskins star set a record the following year for most points scored in a season on kicking alone, with 161. As a further distinction, he was also the last of the straight-ahead kickers.

In 1991 another Redskins kicker scored "only" 149 points but enjoyed the unusual distinction of outscoring one whole team—the 1–15 Indianapolis Colts—all by himself. It was the first time anyone had done that since 1945. Who was this "one-man team"?

The man who set the single-season scoring record in 1960 didn't manage to outscore any teams, but he came close. His 176 points (in 12 games, believe it or not) fell only 1 short of the Cowboys' total and 2 short of the Redskins'—two teams that combined to win one game that year. The scoring champ followed his record-setting season with 146 points in 1961, leading the NFL for the third straight year. Who was the Packers' point-making machine?

This great receiver scored only one touchdown in 1997, but it was enough to make him the first nonkicker ever to score 1,000 points in a career.

Obviously the last man is the career touchdown leader. Can you name the first player to score 100 touchdowns? He called it quits after the 1945 season with a total of 105.

This receiver and kicker is the AFL's career scoring leader. Joining the Patriots after several years in Canada, he led the league five times, with a high of 155 points in 1964.

The league's first scoring leader, however, was not the last man, but a man with no college experience who tallied 123 points in 1960. Two years later he repeated as the scoring champ, this time with 137. Who is this Broncos halfback? Hint: He returned a punt for a touchdown in the AFL's first game, as the Broncos beat the Patriots.

Game 4

1st Quarter

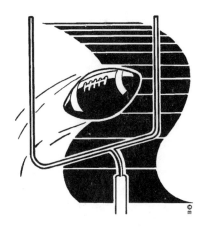

Yesterday's Heroes

 1. In his first five years in the NFL, including the strike-shortened 1982 season, this Falcons standout rushed for 5,772 yards and caught 272 passes. But a preseason knee injury in 1984 short-circuited what might have been a Hall of Fame career. It sidelined him for two years, and though he made a heroic effort at a comeback in 1986, he was just a shell of the player who had gained a combined 2,176 yards three years earlier. Who was this former Auburn star?

 2. A consensus all-pro with the Vikings every year from 1964 through 1970, this 235-pounder was the best of the "greyhound" centers, a breed that died out with the coming of the nose tackle in the 3–4 defense. This 17-year veteran is virtually for-gotten today by most fans, including the Hall of Fame selec-tion committee.

This wide receiver was a marvel of consistency with the Bengals. From 1981 through 1986, excluding the strike season of 1982, he caught 67, 66, 64, 65, and 62 passes and missed 1,000 yards only once—in 1984, when he gained 989. In an eight-year career, all with Cincinnati, he caught a team-record 417 passes. Who was this former Florida Gator?

Our last man caught one pass more than the Bengals' previous team leader, who had retired after the 1984 season. But his pre-decessor retained the team record for receiving yards, with 7,101, and touchdowns, with 53. Can you name this four-time all-pro?

In a two-year period (1962–'63) this Eagles halfback amassed a total of 4,731 yards—and that doesn't include a 99-yard touchdown return of a missed field goal in 1962. In a nine-year career that earned him three trips to the Pro Bowl, he rushed for 3,862 yards, caught passes for 3,399, and returned kickoffs for 4,781 (plus five touchdowns). He spent his final season with the Colts and played on the losing side in Super Bowl III.

In a 10-year career starting in 1939, this guard was a first-team all-pro six times, all of them with the Rams. He finished in 1948 with the 49ers, earning second-team all-AAFC honors. There are many players in the Hall of Fame without his credentials, but these days he's virtually unknown.

Despite missing five games with injuries, this third-year Broncos running back made the all-AFL team in 1969. He re-peated as an all-AFC selection for the next two years and was the NFL's leading rusher in 1971. His last outstanding season was 1973, when he rushed for 979 yards and a league-leading 12 touchdowns. Who is this former Syracuse All-American?

 In his first two seasons with the Lions, this Heisman Trophy winner from Oklahoma gained 2,740 yards rushing and scored 31 touchdowns. He was still going strong when a knee injury ended his career in the middle of the 1984 season. He also did fine work as a receiver out of the backfield.

 Despite the presence of Joe Namath and Len Dawson, this man may have been the top AFL quarterback of the late '60s. He won two MVP Awards while leading his team to consecutive records of 13–1, 12–2, and 12–1–1. The AFL passing leader in 1967, he also topped the AFC in 1970. He spent the first four years of his career backing up Jack Kemp and faded pretty quickly after 1970, but for four years this Notre Dame grad was about as good as anybody.

 This speedster from Baylor was a unanimous all-pro wide receiver in 1958, '59, '61, '62, and '63. The premier deep threat of his era, he played the last three of those seasons with the Giants, but after that injuries and the rapid decline of the team made him just another player. Still, few receivers have ever matched his dominance over a six-year span.

 The Vikings won their first division title in 1968, the same year they chose this tackle from USC with the first pick in the draft. It probably wasn't a coincidence, either, because he turned out to be a great one. An all-pro selection eight years in a row from 1970 through 1977, and a mainstay of four Super Bowl teams (though admittedly they lost all four), he's still waiting for a call from the Hall of Fame.

 This Cardinals running back gained well over 1,000 yards in five of his first six seasons—the only exception being the strike year of 1982. An injury in 1985 curtailed his effectiveness, though, and he spent the next few seasons as a little-used backup. In 1989, by now with a different team, he got a chance to start when Joe Morris was injured, and he made the most of it, rushing for 14 touchdowns and more than 1,000 yards. A year later he was a surprise choice as MVP in the Super Bowl. Who is this resilient star?

There was a great crop of Hall of Fame quarterbacks in the 1950s: Graham, Van Brocklin, Tittle, Layne, and later Unitas. This Rice alumnus wasn't quite in their class, but he wasn't far behind. He spent most of his career with the lowly Packers, leading the league at various times in completions, yardage, and touchdown passes. He also amassed more than 3,000 yards on the ground, an NFL record for QBs (since broken). When he finally got a chance to play with a contender in 1957 with the Lions, all he did was lead them to the championship, throwing for four TDs in the title game. He jumped to Canada in 1960 but returned in 1963 to lead the Chargers to their first championship.

Since the NFL didn't start counting sacks officially until 1982, this Jets defensive end probably lost at least 30 from his lifetime total. The game's best pass rusher at his peak in the early 1980s, he amassed 41 sacks in 1983 and '84 combined.

Game 4

2nd Quarter

Men of Letters

Quite a few players and coaches have written books over the years. (Never mind the fact that most of them had sportswriters as collaborators.) In some cases the books or their authors are famous enough that you won't get much explanation other than the title.

 What Cardinals linebacker from the 1960s raised eyebrows around the NFL with his bitter farewell to football, called *Out of Their League*?

 This Raiders defensive back celebrated his reputation as a hatchet man in *They Call Me Assassin*.

3. One of the NFL's all-time greats produced two books, two decades apart: *Off My Chest* and *Out of Bounds.*

4. What Dolphins running back who was later convicted on drug charges told his story in *Against the Grain*?

5. A Utah All-American who failed in trials with the Giants and the Jets in the early '60s wrote an account of his aborted career in *Fourth and One.*

6. More than two decades later, a Hall of Fame coach used *Fourth and One* as the title of his own book.

7. The Packers' dynasty in the '60s was described by one of its mainstays in *Instant Replay.*

8. What running back created a stir when he "came out of the closet" in a much-publicized book that was the first of its kind? He came closest to regular duty with the 49ers, with whom he broke in, in 1964, but also saw significant service with the Lions and Redskins in a career that lasted through 1972. No title this time, because it contains his name.

9. What Super Bowl MVP told his story in *Quarterblack*?

10. *They Call Me Dirty* was written by a guard who put his no-holds-barred style of play to good use with the Cardinals, the Saints, and the Bills.

11. A cocky rookie aired his opinions about his teammates with the Jets in *Just Give Me the Damn Ball!*.

This wide receiver with the Cowboys and Rams told of his personal struggles off the field in *When All the Laughter Died in Sorrows*.

 Two years before he hung up his cleats, a Hall of Fame quarterback looked back on his long career in *I Pass!*.

 Best known for clotheslining a fan who had the temerity to run onto the field and snatch the football, this Colts linebacker's book was aptly titled *Keep Off My Turf*.

 What outstanding pass rusher who earned Super Bowl rings with the 49ers and the Cowboys told his story in *All the Rage?*

 A two-time coach of the year, once with the Rams and once with the Redskins, used one of his favorite slogans as the title of his book, *The Future Is Now*.

 What all-pro defensive tackle with the Lions was the author of *Even Big Guys Cry?*

 A Dallas linebacker known for his outrageous antics wrote *Out of Control*.

Game 4

3rd Quarter

Shooting Stars

 A part-time back for most of his first six years, this Notre Dame product gained 1,169 yards on the ground from 1990 through 1995 with four different teams. But in 1996 an early-season injury to Tim Biakabutuka gave him a chance, and he took advantage of it, rushing for 1,120 yards and leading the Carolina Panthers to a 12–4 record.

 Not surprisingly, the highest passer ratings for a single season were generally compiled by some of the greatest quarterbacks: Baugh, Luckman, Marino, Montana, Young. The major exception is this Penn State alumnus who posted a rating (figured retroactively) of 110.4 in 1960 for the Browns. It wasn't a total fluke, since he repeated as the passing leader in 1961, but after that he had only two more seasons as a regular, and only one good one. Last seen with the Giants for a single game in 1969.

The season record for most "touches"—that is, rushes and receptions—is held by a Tampa Bay back who carried the ball a record 407 times in 1984 and also caught 85 passes. The result was 13 touchdowns and more than 2,200 yards. Amazingly, he was almost as busy the next season, with 365 carries (for 1,300 yards) and 53 receptions. Though he was a pretty solid back for most of the '80s, he never again came close to that level of performance. Who is this workhorse?

Few people will remember the two guys who finished second and third in rushing in 1955 behind NFL leader Alan Ameche. One gained 859 yards for the Packers; the other picked up 824 for the Browns, for whom he also punted for several seasons, though that wasn't one of them. Those 1955 yardage figures represented more than one-third of each man's career total. Give yourself full credit if you know either one.

In 1983 this fourth-year Kansas City quarterback passed for 4,348 yards and 24 touchdowns with a league-leading 346 completions and earned his only trip to the Pro Bowl. A broken thumb sidelined him for half of the next season, and though he played regularly through 1987, he never came close to duplicating his 1983 numbers.

When the Redskins won their first Super Bowl after the 1982 season, they did it without Art Monk, who was hurt just before the playoffs began. His little-known replacement picked up the slack with 15 catches in playoff games for 244 yards and five TDs. He started the next season the same way, catching 25 passes in the early going before Monk returned. Over the rest of his five-year career he caught a total of 10 passes, including playoffs. Who is this super sub? Hint: Howard

Cosell was referring to him when he made his infamous "little monkey" remark.

A starter for only three of his seven years in the NFL, this Eagles quarterback and punter enjoyed one magical day in 1954 when he tied a record with seven touchdown passes in a 49–21 win over the Redskins. He finished in 1956 with a career total of 61 TD passes.

Fifteen years later, a Vikings quarterback matched the last man's mark when he victimized the Colts' secondary for seven TDs in a 52–14 victory. He threw only 33 more TD passes in a four-year NFL career; to be fair, though, he also had 136 scoring tosses in Canada. Who was this former California Golden Bear?

A second-year Broncos running back was one of the big surprises of the 1974 season, leading the NFL with 1,407 yards rushing and making virtually every all-pro team. Injured for most of the following year, he bounced back with another 1,000-yard season in 1976, but it was his last year as a featured back. He hung on through 1980, still effective in a reduced role, but never came close to repeating his great sophomore season.

What college basketball star made a name for himself as a 49ers rookie in 1957 when he and Y. A. Tittle devised the "Alley Oop" play, in which Tittle would loft a high pass and our man would outjump the defensive back for the ball? He actually had his best season in 1961, after Tittle was gone, when he caught 55 passes for 1,032 yards.

When this rookie carried 22 times for a record 204 yards in Washington's 42–10 win over Denver in Super Bowl XXII, it was 78 yards more than he gained in the whole regular season. Given a starting job a year later, he lost it after a few games and was finished after that season, except for one game with the Cowboys in 1990. Who is this one-game wonder?

As a rookie tailback with the Cardinals in 1942, he set a record by throwing 295 passes, but the results weren't impressive: six touchdowns, 27 interceptions, and an average of 4.6 yards per throw. After three years in the service, he returned in 1946 as Otto Graham's backup in the Browns' inaugural season. A year later, having moved to Baltimore, he led the AAFC in attempts and completions and trailed only Graham in yardage. But Y. A. Tittle's arrival in 1948 made him expendable, and he spent his final season on the New York Yankees' bench. Who are we talking about?

From 1971 through 1973 this 49ers tight end caught 139 passes and made three trips to the Pro Bowl. In six other seasons, three with the 49ers and three with the Raiders, he caught only 29 passes altogether—a total he matched in 1975 with the Philadelphia Bell of the WFL. Who is this Penn State star?

A little-used backup wide receiver with the Browns, he caught 12 passes in his first four seasons. In 1968 he joined the 49ers and turned into an all-pro, catching 71 passes to lead the NFL. He caught a mere 17 a year later, then moved on to the Giants, where he enjoyed a resurgence with 50 receptions in 1970, but again it didn't last. He drifted to the Redskins in mid-1971 and was last seen with the Oilers in 1973. Who is this Grambling product?

Game 4

4th Quarter

Black Pioneers

 An easy one to start with: What Hall of Fame tackle became the modern NFL's first black head coach in 1989, the same year he was inducted into the Hall?

 I used the term "modern NFL" in the last question because the league had its first black coach in its second season, 1921. An All-American from Brown, he was co-coach and star half-back of the Akron Pros, who finished third, a year after winning the 1920 championship. He played in the NFL through 1926, also serving as player-coach with Milwaukee and Hammond.

One of the last man's best assets in 1921 with Akron was a big end from Rutgers, a two-time All-American who soon earned recognition as one of the league's best. He moved to Milwaukee in 1922, his last season. Despite his considerable football talent, he's much better remembered today as a singer and actor (star of *The Emperor Jones*) who suffered during the McCarthy era for his Marxist beliefs.

Of the blacks who played in the NFL before the color line, this tackle from Iowa was probably the best. In a 10-year career from 1922 through 1931 he was a consistent first- or second-team all-pro selection. He played through 1926 with the Rock Island Independents, then spent his last years with the Chicago Cardinals.

In 1968 this Broncos rookie became the first black quarterback to play a season as a regular, passing decently and showing real ability as a scrambler, rushing for 308 yards and averaging 7.5 yards per carry. Traded to the Bills in 1969, he moved to wide receiver, and in 1970 he was an all-pro, catching 57 passes for 1,036 yards. Later a member of Miami's back-to-back champs in 1972 and '73, he was last seen with the Patriots in 1976.

A decent number of blacks played in the NFL in the 1920s and early '30s, but after 1933 the league instituted an "unofficial" color line—that is, no one admitted it, but it was definitely there. The league's two black players from 1933 were not invited back. One, a tackle from Duquesne who saw action with Pittsburgh, was playing his only NFL season. The other, a tailback from Oregon, played for the Cardinals in 1932 and '33, and kept popping up over the next eight years with various minor league and independent teams, including the New York Brown Bombers, an all-black team that appeared in 1935. Take full credit if you can name one of them.

The color line was broken in 1946 when the Rams, just arrived in Los Angeles, signed two stars from the Hollywood Bears of the Pacific Coast Football League. One, a tailback from UCLA, had been one of the best players in the professional ranks since 1940. A knee injury curtailed his effectiveness with the Rams, but he led the NFL with a 7.4-yard rushing average in 1947, including a 92-yard run, and played effectively through 1948. The other trailblazer, also a UCLA man, played little at end in 1946, then went off to Canada, where he starred for a couple more seasons. Later he returned to Hollywood, this time as an actor, and played supporting roles in quite a few movies, including *Spartacus*.

 The AAFC was a new league in 1946, so you couldn't really say it had established a color line, but some in the league weren't happy when the Browns signed two blacks. Both turned out to be great players, helping Paul Brown's team dominate the league for the whole of its four-year existence. One, a guard from Ohio State, was named to the Hall of Fame in 1977. The other, a fullback, was inducted nine years earlier, and at least one noted expert considers him the best player ever, at any position.

 In 1963 the Giants made him the NFL's first black assistant coach, but he's in the Hall of Fame for his career as a defensive back. In 14 years with the Giants and Packers, he picked off 79 passes and was one of the game's best punt returners.

 He's usually listed as the first black quarterback, and he certainly had the right name for the job, but this Michigan State product threw only eight passes with the Bears in 1953, his only season in the NFL.

 Actually, another black QB preceded the last man. Signed by the Los Angeles Dons of the AAFC in 1949 after a college career with Indiana, he split time with Glenn Dobbs at tailback in his rookie year and passed for 790 yards. Moving into the

NFL with the New York Yanks in 1950, he shifted to halfback. But when George Ratterman jumped to Canada in 1951 the Yanks were left without an established QB, and for the next three years several candidates were shuttled in and out as the team itself was shuttled from New York to Dallas to Baltimore. Our man played enough time at quarterback to throw 151 passes from 1951 through 1953 and was also the team's top rusher in 1951.

 By 1961 the Redskins were the only NFL team that had yet to employ a black player. But pressure from the federal government finally forced owner George Preston Marshall to integrate the team, and in 1962 four blacks played for the Redskins. The most prominent was a former Cleveland Browns halfback who switched to wide receiver that season and led the league in receiving. Today he's a member of the Hall of Fame.

 A landmark in integration occurred in 1954, when all of the NFL's top five rushers were black. The top two men, both from the 49ers, are in the Hall of Fame; the next two, both from the Rams, were stars in their own right. The No. 5 man, however, played only three years, all with the Browns, and never gained as many as 200 yards in a season thereafter. How many of them can you name?

 In 1974 this Grambling alumnus became the first black quarterback to start a playoff game, calling the signals for the Rams against the Redskins. He was a starter for four seasons, the last with the Chargers in 1977.

 A few years later, another Grambling product enjoyed a five-year run as the starting QB for Tampa Bay. In the process, he led the Bucs to the NFC championship game and became the first black passer to throw for 3,000 yards in a season. After a sojourn in the USFL, he returned to the NFL as a backup but moved in as a starter during the 1987 season and became the first black

QB to start in the Super Bowl. He didn't do too badly, either, winning the MVP Award.

The first black QB to start in the Super Bowl *could* have been another fellow, who spent a good part of the 1974 season as the Steelers' starter. When Terry Bradshaw came back from an injury, though, he sent this Tennessee State product to the sidelines. His NFL career was over a year later, and he was last seen in 1983 with Washington in the USFL.

Game 5

1st Quarter

All in the Family

 Senior was a solid defensive lineman who played 14 years in the NFL and started for the Colts in Super Bowls III and V; Junior spent 10 years as a linebacker with the Chargers, finishing in 1992. What's the name they shared?

 These two brothers from Niagara Falls, New York, were teammates in 1965 and '66 with the Toronto Rifles of the Continental League. Earlier, Charlie, a guard, had spent four seasons in the AFL, three with the Patriots, earning all-AFL recognition in 1961. Jim, the younger brother, played one year with the Giants and two with the Vikings as a linebacker and defensive end. All you need is their last name.

Three brothers from Moss Point, Mississippi, made it to the NFL in the 1980s. George had one fine season with the Colts in 1985, rushing for 716 yards, more than half his total for a six-year career. Nathan rushed for 339 yards with Tampa Bay in 1986, his only season. Otis, also a running back by trade, spent most of his five-year career on special teams but played in two Super Bowls with the Redskins and earned a championship ring. Do you know their family name?

Each of this pair of siblings had seasons as a league leader. The elder, a fullback and kicker from Minnesota, led in scoring in 1934 and 1937. The younger, a fullback from Drake, led in rushing in 1941. Need more? The scoring leader played his whole eight-year career with the Bears; the rushing leader played six of his nine years with the Brooklyn Dodgers.

As a two-way end with the Bears from 1937 through 1946, dad played in six championship games, four times on the winning side. He won another title in his first year as a head coach with Detroit in 1957. In 1966 he took over the AFL's first expansion team, in Miami, where his son and namesake served as a punter and quarterback. It was Junior's first and only season in the professional ranks, but Senior held onto the Dolphins job until Don Shula replaced him in 1970.

These two brothers were offensive linemen for NFC East rivals throughout the '80s. The better-known sibling, a center, played 14 years with the Redskins and was one of the original Hogs. The other, a guard and tackle, played 10 years with the Cardinals, the last in 1988. Who are they?

From 1984 through 1987 these brothers were teammates with the 49ers. The elder was an offensive tackle who played his entire 14-year career in San Francisco; his kid brother was a linebacker who broke in with the Chicago Blitz in the USFL.

One of the greatest stars of the early years was a Hall of Fame halfback who teamed up with his brother, an end, with the Bears from 1929 through 1931. Their parents named them Harold and Garland, but the Hall of Famer went by a different name.

 These two brothers from BYU both played in the USFL with the Philadelphia Stars, but for one it was a stepping stone and for the other it was a swan song. The elder, an offensive tackle and guard, had played with five teams from 1976 through 1981 and called it quits after the 1984 season. The younger, a center, moved to the NFL when the USFL folded and played on Super Bowl winners with the Giants and the 49ers. Who are these two linemen?

 This father-and-son team combined to catch more than 600 passes in the NFL. Dad hauled in 281 for the Browns from 1952 through 1963, 50 of them for touchdowns; his offspring snagged 323 for the Oilers and Cowboys from 1978 through 1987.

 The elder of these siblings was the Browns' leading rusher in the 1955 championship game; his kid brother was a mainstay on the Cleveland defensive line when the Browns won their next title in 1964. Earlier, the latter had played in six title games with the Giants but wound up on the short end of the score five times. Can you name these two Maryland alumni?

 These two brothers both played in the Pro Bowl. The elder, a defensive back, played with five different teams in a nine-year career and finished with Detroit in 1973, where he teamed up with his sibling, a halfback who was ending his own seven-year career, all of it with the Lions. Hint: The younger brother later had two sons who played briefly in the NFL, with the Lions and the Rams, respectively.

For the first five seasons of the Buccaneers' existence, the Tampa Bay defense featured two brothers, both of whom played college ball at Oklahoma. One of them, an end, was the defensive Player of the Year in 1979 and is now a member of the Hall of Fame.

 Willie, a wide receiver from Jackson State, was a member of the Colts when they lost the 1964 NFL title game and Super Bowl III. Moving to Miami in 1970, he missed the Colts' victory in Super Bowl V, then returned to Baltimore for his finale in 1971. His younger brother Gloster, another wide receiver from Jackson State, had a less distinguished career but was a member of two Super Bowl winners: the 1969 Chiefs and the 1971 Cowboys. A third brother, Tom, caught a single pass for the Patriots in 1969. What's their family name?

Game 5

2nd Quarter

Stand-Ins

1. This 42-year-old kicker and backup quarterback had an amazing stretch in 1970 during which he brought the Raiders from behind in the final minutes to win or tie five consecutive games. He was named the AFC Player of the Year despite throwing only 55 passes and scoring only 84 points. Who is this geriatric wonder?

2. Sterling Sharpe's forced retirement after the 1994 season left the Packers shorthanded at wide receiver, but a fourth-year pro stepped up and had a season worthy of the departed star, catching 102 passes for 1,497 yards and 13 touchdowns. Who was this pass catcher from South Carolina (coincidentally, the same school Sharpe attended)?

Trailing the Oilers 35–3 in the third quarter of a playoff game on January 3, 1993, the Bills staged the greatest comeback in NFL history and finally won in overtime, 41–38. Perhaps the most amazing thing about it is that the Bills' starting quarterback, Jim Kelly, was sidelined with an injury; Buffalo's great rally was accomplished by a backup who threw for four touchdowns. In college the same QB had led Maryland to an equally historic comeback victory over the Miami Hurricanes. Who was this comeback king?

 A similar scenario occurred 11 years earlier when the Dolphins, trailing the Chargers 24–0 after the first quarter, came all the way back to take a 38–31 lead in the fourth quarter, only to fall victim to a game-tying touchdown pass by Dan Fouts and a game-winning field goal in overtime by Rolf Benirschke. Who was the backup QB who came off the Miami bench to lead this ill-fated comeback, throwing for 403 yards and four TDs?

 When Bill Dudley forced the Steelers to trade him to Detroit before the 1947 season started, things didn't look good in Pittsburgh. But Dudley's backup stepped in and led the team to a first-place tie with the Eagles, to whom they lost in a divisional playoff. Who was the former SMU tailback who exceeded Dudley's 1946 totals in rushing and passing yardage?

 When Boyd Dowler was injured at the start of Super Bowl I, the Packers replaced him with a 10-year veteran from Tulane who had once been Green Bay's top receiver but was now a little-used backup, having caught only four passes in the regular season. On top of that, he'd been out all night before the game, not expecting that he'd have to play. But he turned in a great performance, scoring the first touchdown in Super Bowl history on a terrific one-handed catch and finishing the day with seven receptions for 138 yards and a pair of TDs. Who was this super sub?

 With Johnny Unitas sidelined by an elbow injury, the 1968 Colts acquired a veteran quarterback who filled in so well that he led the NFL in passing while Baltimore rolled to a 13–1 record before falling to the Jets in the Super Bowl. Four years later the Dolphins lost Bob Griese from midseason until the second half of the AFC championship game, but his replacement topped the AFC in passing and drove the Dolphins to an undefeated season. The kicker is that we're not talking about two backups here—just one man who gave coach Don Shula two great seasons. Who was he?

Just days before the 1939 championship game against Green Bay, the Giants learned that head coach Steve Owen's mother had died and that he would be unavailable for the game. His place on the sidelines was taken by an assistant coach who had been a mainstay of the Packers' three-time champs of 1929–31. Who was this former fullback, who never got another chance as a head coach after the Giants lost the title game 27–0?

Frankie Sinkwich was the MVP in 1944 as he led the Lions to a 6–3–1 record. Though Sinkwich entered the service during the off-season, Detroit improved slightly to 7–3 in 1945. One of the keys to the Lions' success was a UCLA product who filled in admirably for the departed star. A year later, with the Los Angeles Dons, he averaged 8.4 yards per carry to lead the AAFC. Who was he?

While Archie Manning sat out the 1976 season with a shoulder injury, the Saints "improved" from 2–12 to 4–10, thanks to the arrival of new coach Hank Stram and rookie running backs Chuck Muncie and Tony Galbreath. The extra two wins couldn't have been the work of the two quarterbacks who handled the job in Manning's absence and combined for eight touchdown passes and an average of less than six yards per pass. Who were they?

What veteran punter/kicker took over the Browns' kicking job in 1960 when Lou Groza tried retirement for a year? Our man finished fourth in the NFL in scoring and hung around to do the Browns' punting when Groza returned in 1961. In a 15-year career that started in Washington and ended in Philadelphia, he scored 977 points and averaged 42.6 yards per punt.

 When Phil Simms went down late in the 1990 season, the Giants inserted this backup from West Virginia and upset the 49ers in the NFC title game and the Bills in the Super Bowl. Elevated to the starter's job by virtue of his performance in the playoffs, he took much of the blame when the Giants fell to an 8–8 record the following year.

 Off to a 1–3–1 start in 1961, the Oilers fired head coach Lou Rymkus. Under his replacement the team immediately began a streak of nine straight wins to end the regular season, then capped it with another victory in the championship game. The new coach jumped ship in the off-season, taking an NFL job with the rebuilding Cardinals. He didn't do badly in St. Louis, where he got as high as second place in 1964, and when he returned to Houston, he guided the Oilers to their last Eastern Division title in 1967. But he never topped that great "relief" job he did in 1961.

 Finishing the 1965 season tied with the Packers for first place in the West, the Colts faced a playoff game with Johnny Unitas and his backup, Gary Cuozzo, both hurt. Don Shula entrusted the quarterback job to a versatile halfback who called the plays from a list written on his wristband. The Colts lost in overtime, but this last-minute fill-in went on to a fine career, gaining more than 7,500 yards rushing and receiving—but only 246 passing. Who is he?

 Statistically speaking, this man had the two best seasons ever by a backup quarterback. In 1987 he threw 10 touchdown passes without an interception and had a passer rating of 120.8; just two years later he matched that rating by completing 69.6 percent of his throws for an average gain of 10.9 yards per pass. I won't tell you anything more, because he's still playing—and playing well.

The Oilers went into San Diego for a second-round playoff after the 1979 season without the services of quarterback Dan Pastorini and running back Earl Campbell. But they escaped with a 17–14 victory and advanced to the AFC championship game, thanks in part to fine efforts by the fill-ins for their offensive stars. The running back, a starter before Campbell arrived and again with the Giants in the 1980s, rushed for 67 yards and caught 4 passes; the backup QB, an All-American from BYU, completed 10 of 19 passes, including a 47-yard game-winner to Mike Renfro. Do you remember them?

Game 5

3rd
Quarter

Milestones

1. In the early days of pro football, quite a few players declined to wear helmets. More and more saw the light over the years, though, and by 1941 there was only one man in the NFL who insisted on playing au naturel. A fine end with the Bears, he disdained a helmet for his first five years in the league, from 1937 through 1941. He went into the service after that, and by the time he returned in 1944, the league had made helmets mandatory, so he was forced to cover up for his final three years. Who was this bare-headed marvel?

2. When our last man joined the Bears in 1937, he replaced a Hall of Fame end who was probably the next-to-last to play with-

out a helmet. The Hall of Famer moved on to the Eagles, for whom he played three years before retiring after the 1939 season. (He returned for a few games in 1943 when the war caused a shortage of players.) Some of you probably thought he was the answer to the last question; if so, you'll have no trouble with this one.

 The last to play without a face mask was a wide receiver who's now a member of the Hall of Fame. He had his best years with the Eagles in the late 1950s and early '60s. Who is this former Oklahoma star?

 On Thanksgiving Day, 1929, the Chicago Cardinals routed the Bears 40–6. What made the game particularly notable was the fact that the Cardinals' fullback scored all of their points, setting a single-game record that still stands. Who was this Hall of Famer?

 The first soccer-style kicker in pro football, he broke in with Buffalo in 1964 and bowed out 10 years later, having scored 863 points and blazed a trail for many others to follow. In addition, his signing by the Giants in 1966 escalated the war between the leagues and forced both sides to get serious about a merger.

 What quarterback set an NFL record with 33 touchdown passes in 1962, then broke his own record when he threw 36 more a year later?

 This second-year wide receiver from UCLA burned the Saints for a record 336 yards on 15 receptions in a 1989 game. Actually, that game brought down his per-catch average; for the season he averaged a whopping 26 yards for each reception. He followed with another terrific season in 1990 and remained a solid receiver through 1994. He may not have been faster than lightning, but who is the man who made the Rams' long passing game go?

In nine seasons with the Chiefs he caught 377 passes, but he's mainly remembered for one magical game—the season finale in 1985 against the Chargers, when he caught eight for 309 yards, breaking a 40-year-old record for yardage in a single game. For the season he averaged 21.9 yards per catch and scored 10 touchdowns; a year later he scored 11.

The record the last man broke had belonged to an end for the Cleveland Rams who caught 10 passes for 303 yards against the Lions in 1945. One of the true standouts of his era, he retired after the 1947 season as the No. 2 man on the career receiving list. In 1945 he even managed to gain more yards than Don Hutson, thanks in large part to that big game in Detroit.

What Vikings receiver caught 10 passes for a playoff–record 227 yards in an upset victory over the 49ers following the 1987 season? He also carried once on a reverse, for 30 yards. A week earlier he had returned six punts for 143 yards, including an 84-yard touchdown, as the Vikings routed the Saints in the wild-card game. Still need a hint? Ok, he played his college ball at Michigan.

A Kansas City linebacker set the single-game record for sacks when he registered seven in a game against the Seahawks in 1990. Can you name this perennial Pro Bowl selection?

If the NFL had been counting sacks in the 1950s, though, the record would probably belong to a Philadelphia defensive end who had an incredible afternoon against the Giants in 1952. His sack total for that day is variously estimated at anywhere from 12 to 17! Who is this two-time all-pro who was nicknamed "Wild Man"?

The first man to average 100 yards rushing per game did it in 1947—and it wasn't Steve Van Buren. Our man also passed for more than 100 yards a game, and nobody else has ever done both in the same season. He threw for 14 touchdowns and scored a record 19 himself. In his spare time, he punted 46 times for a 42-yard average, ran back kickoffs for 593 yards, and averaged 27 yards on six punt returns. It all adds up to one of the best all-around seasons anyone ever had, but despite his heroic efforts, his team fell just short of the AAFC championship, losing out to the Browns.

Jim Brown, as you might expect, was the first to average 100 yards a game in the NFL. He did it seven times, the first coming 11 years after our last man turned the trick. The next two to cross the 100-yards-a-game barrier did it in 1962 and 1966, respectively. Both were bruising fullbacks; one played for an NFL dynasty that was winning its second straight championship, the other for a Boston Patriots team that finished second in the AFL's Eastern Division. They both finished their careers in Louisiana—the former with the Saints, the latter with Shreveport in the WFL. Who were they?

Game 5

4th Quarter

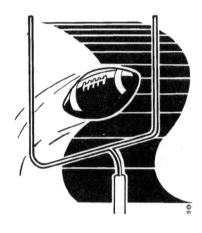

Gridiron Tragedy

1. In 1977 he was the Patriots' best receiver, with 39 catches for 657 yards. But a brutal hit by Oakland's Jack Tatum in a 1978 preseason game left him paralyzed, and he never played, or even walked, again.

2. The AFC Rookie of the Year in 1981, he rushed for 1,121 yards with the Chiefs. After a sophomore season marred by injuries, he died in the summer of 1983 while trying to save three children from drowning.

3. The Lions' first pick in the 1996 draft, this linebacker quickly became one of their defensive mainstays. But in the final regular-season game of 1997 he suffered a career-ending neck injury. His life hung in the balance for a few minutes, but in the off-season he was making good strides toward resuming a normal life.

After breaking in with the 49ers in 1951, this offensive lineman from South Carolina went into the service for two years. Discharged in 1954, he hooked on with the Redskins but didn't make it all the way through the season, dying of a heart attack on December 5, 1954.

A fourth-year defensive lineman with the Oilers committed suicide in December 1993. Can you name this troubled soul from Notre Dame?

In the AFL's inaugural season, the Chargers' leading receiver died late in the year as a result of a diabetes attack. Though he had seen a little action with the Bears in 1958, it was his first season as a regular in the professional ranks.

A consensus all-pro every year from 1955 through 1958 with the Redskins, this great defensive end got a chance to play in his hometown when he was traded to the Rams in 1959. But a rare muscle disease called myasthenia gravis ended his career after the 1960 season, and he died in 1965 at the age of 39.

In the late 1960s he was Gale Sayers's running mate and best friend with the Bears. But he was diagnosed with cancer after the 1969 season and died the following summer. The moving story of their friendship was later told in a bestselling book and a hit TV movie.

In the days when players took off-season jobs to supplement their income from football, a three-year starter at safety for the Browns was killed in an off-season construction accident in 1963. Do you remember him?

This defensive tackle from Miami was just hitting his stride with the Eagles when he was killed in a car accident before the 1992 season. A five-year veteran, he was coming off two straight all-pro seasons.

 The Redskins drafted this Heisman Trophy winner from Syracuse before the 1962 season and shipped him to the Browns for Bobby Mitchell. But it was soon discovered that he was suffering from leukemia, and he died without ever playing a down in the NFL.

 This offensive lineman joined the Lions along with Barry Sanders. In 1991, his third year, Detroit was on its way to its first winning record since 1983 when a serious injury in a late-season game ended his career and left him paralyzed. Do you remember the stoic hero who gave the crowd and his teammates a thumbs-up sign while being carried from the field?

 A year later a fourth-year defensive end with the Jets suffered the same fate as the last man. With great determination he worked to regain limited movement, and his battle back was later made into a TV movie.

 A three-time participant in the AFL all-star game as a member of the Chargers, this linebacker was snapped up by the Bengals in the 1968 expansion draft. He played regularly for Cincinnati that year but died of a pulmonary embolism on the opening day of the 1969 season. Who was this USC alumnus?

 This defensive back from UCLA was just settling in with the Browns when he died of a cocaine overdose before the 1986 season.

Game 6

1st Quarter

Coaching Carousel

In seven years as the Giants' head coach, he compiled a regular-season record of 53–27–4. His teams reached the NFL title game three times, winning in 1956 and losing in 1958 and '59. Who was this little-remembered leader?

Perhaps the reason for the last man's lack of recognition is that he was overshadowed by his offensive and defensive co-ordinators, who went on to become two of the game's greatest head coaches. (The offensive assistant's later teams were known for their impregnable defense, and the defensive assistant's teams were known for their innovative offense.) Who were these able assistants?

Another highly successful but largely forgotten coach is the man who succeeded Paul Brown with Cleveland in 1963. In an eight-year career he won five division titles and took the Browns to four NFL championship games, winning it all in 1964. And even Paul Brown himself would have been proud of our man's 76–34–2 regular-season record.

The first coach to win four championships, he turned the trick with Canton in 1922 and '23, Cleveland in 1924, and Frankford in 1926. As a player he may have been the best end of the 1920s, and as a coach his career record was a sparkling 58–16–7.

Here's an easy one: Who's the only coach to win four Super Bowls?

That last record is misleading, because it presumes that winning the Super Bowl is somehow different from simply winning the NFL title. Actually, what we should ask is which coach has won the most championships? As it happens, two men are tied with six apiece. The greatest team-builders of the NFL's first two decades, they won their first titles in 1921 and 1929, respectively; the more famous of the two won his last in 1963. Who are these two giants?

To get back to the Super Bowl, though, let's consider a much less publicized accomplishment: Who's the only coach to take his team to the Super Bowl six times? Hint: He did it with two different teams, and he lost four of the six games.

When Bud Grant stepped down as the Vikings' coach after an 8–8 season in 1983, he was replaced by a 38-year-old assistant whose aggressive style grated on players who were used to the laid-back Grant. The result was a disastrous 3–13 season, at the end of which Grant agreed to come back for one more year to right the sinking ship. Who was Minnesota's ill-fated leader?

As the first coach of the 49ers, he made a habit of finishing second: six times in nine years in San Francisco. In 1958 he took over a poor Philadelphia team, and a year later the Eagles improved to—what else?—second place. In 1960 the Eagles went all the way, winning the NFL title against the Packers' budding dynasty, and their perennial runner-up coach went out on top.

His teams never reached the Super Bowl, but during the 1970s he was known as perhaps the game's most innovative offensive coach. He was the NFL's Coach of the Year with the Cardinals in 1974, and he reached the AFC championship game twice in a row with the Chargers in the early '80s.

The Lions played in three straight championship games in the early '50s and won two of them. They just missed another title trip in 1956, and expectations for the next season were high when their head coach stunned the football world by leaving the team during training camp. Signed immediately by Pittsburgh, he never could get the Steelers over the hump, despite near misses in 1962 and '63.

And what about the Lions, the team our last man left in the lurch in 1957? All they did was win another championship, their third of the decade and last to date. Who was the replacement coach who took them all the way?

This former all-pro linebacker got his start as a head coach in 1974 with the WFL's Florida Blazers and took them all the way to the championship game, where they lost by a single point. In 1977 he took the Bears to the playoffs after a 14-year drought; seven years later he led the Houston Gamblers to a 13–5 record and a division title in the USFL. Back in the NFL again, he guided the Oilers to 11 straight wins in 1993 en route to their fourth straight playoff appearance. A 1–5 record in the playoffs has tended to obscure the fact that he was named NFC Coach of the Year in 1976 and '79.

14 Another coach whose playoff losses have overshadowed his regular-season successes is this former Buffalo linebacker who's taken three teams to the AFC championship game but come up on the short end each time. In 1995 and '97 his teams went 13–3 but suffered heartbreaking losses in their first playoff game. Who is this hard-luck leader, the AFC's Coach of the Year in 1986?

Game 6

2nd Quarter

Notorious

The Colts took this Ohio State quarterback in the first round of the 1982 draft. But he showed little, lost the starting job to a less-heralded rookie, Mike Pagel, and was suspended during the off-season for running up big gambling losses. He returned for two more seasons with the Colts but never managed to earn a starting job, and was sent packing after the '85 season.

Though the Oilers finished the 1993 season with 11 straight wins, the team was plagued by turmoil in the coaching staff that culminated when the defensive coordinator threw a punch at his offensive counterpart on the sidelines in a game that was televised around the country. Who was the defensive coach, who had already shown a tendency to rub people the wrong way in previous stints with two other teams? And for real experts, who was the offensive coach, who got his shot as a head coach in 1997?

Virtually booed out of New York after three years with the Giants in the mid-1970s, this quarterback has one of the worst playoff passing records of anyone with a substantial number of attempts. On the other hand, he did take two different teams to the Super Bowl, and in 1977 with the Broncos he was chosen as the AFC Player of the Year. Can you name him?

What rookie quarterback set a record with 21 fumbles in 1996? Since it was so recently, I won't tell you his team, but I'll add that he played college ball at Michigan State.

When Chicago sportswriter Arch Ward announced the formation of the All-America Football Conference in August 1945, the NFL commissioner responded that the new league should "first get a ball, then make a schedule, and then play a game." Who was the man whose flippant remark gave the AAFC a rallying cry? Hint: By the time the new league had become a reality and a financial thorn in the NFL's side, he was no longer the commissioner.

After a great season with the Packers as a kickoff returner in 1971, this running back got his shot at a full-time job with Atlanta a year later, and in the fourth quarter of the season's final game he became the Falcons' first 1,000-yard rusher. But a few plays later he was spilled for a loss, and he ended the season with 995. He had to wait until 1975 to finally get his 1,000-yard season.

In 1988, speaking in front of a Senate committee, this Redskins pass rusher tearfully revealed that he had gone through college at Oklahoma State despite being functionally illiterate.

Three years later, by now with Tampa Bay after a couple of drug-related suspensions, he was banned from the NFL after failing his fourth drug test.

The Jets were leading the Raiders 32–29 in a late-season 1968 game when NBC cut away from the broadcast in the final minute to avoid delaying the 7 P.M. start of a children's movie. Unfortunately for the network, the Raiders scored two touchdowns in the final seconds for an improbable 43–32 win, and angry football fans lit up the phones at NBC. What was the movie that indirectly caused such a fuss?

In a 1964 game against the 49ers, this Vikings defensive end scooped up a fumble in San Francisco territory and "returned" it 66 yards the wrong way, into his own end zone, then tossed the ball into the stands for a 49ers safety. Luckily for him, the Vikings won, and he went on to play a record 282 consecutive games.

Leading the Eagles 17–14 late in a 1995 game, this team surprised everyone by going for it on fourth-and-one inside its own 30-yard line. The play failed, but the officials ruled that the two-minute warning had occurred before the snap, giving the offense a reprieve. Incredibly, they chose to go for it again, and another play was stopped short of a first down. The Eagles tied the game with a field goal and went on to win 20–17. What was the team they beat, and who was the head coach whose decision was a Monday-morning quarterback's dream?

One of the key plays of the 1945 championship game occurred in the first quarter, when this quarterback's pass hit the goal post and fell back into his own end zone. Under the rules of the time, it was a safety, and those two points turned out to be the difference, giving the Rams a 15–14 victory.

What quarterback missed several weeks of the 1997 season with a broken hand suffered when he got into a scuffle with a TV broadcaster who called him a baby? And who was the broadcaster, a former quarterback in his first year behind the microphones?

The Bears won the Western Division title in 1956 by defeating the Lions in the season finale, 38–21. The key play came early in the game when Bobby Layne was kayoed by a very late hit from what Chicago defensive end?

Despite the fact that this team had averaged 70,000 fans per home game for years, the owner announced early one season that he was moving to a city that would build him a new stadium with public money. This desertion of fans who had supported the team for five decades outraged people around the league, and the team, considered a possible Super Bowl contender, collapsed after a 3–1 start and lost 10 of its last 12 games. What team and what owner are we talking about?

This defensive lineman and linebacker was a teammate of O. J. Simpson in college at USC and in the professional ranks with the Bills and the 49ers. A decent but unremarkable player in his nine-year NFL career, he achieved brief notoriety during the height of the Simpson melodrama in 1994 as the driver of the white Bronco in what must have been the most-watched car chase in history.

Game 6

3rd Quarter

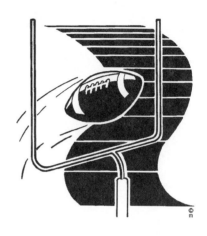

Nicknames

1. Choo-Choo (either of two: one, New York Giants 1947–50; the other, Washington 1950, 1952–54)

2. Cookie

3. Crazy Legs

4. Deacon (two possibilities: one very famous, one less so)

5. The Diesel

The Dutchman

 Flipper

 Eggs

 Frenchy

 Father

 Fuzzy

 Fats

 The Galloping Ghost

 Flea

 Goose

Game 6

4th Quarter

Odds and Ends

1. This pass rusher par excellence has posted sack totals in double figures every year since his sophomore season—except 1991, when a knee injury limited him to five games and just 1.5 sacks. But even with that one aberration, his career total is still the second highest since this became an official category. Who is this great defensive end?

2. When it came to choosing a quarterback, the NFL's two expansion teams of 1976 were at the opposite ends of the spectrum. Tampa Bay's starter was a veteran playing the final season of an undistinguished 10-year career; Seattle's was a rookie who hung around until 1987. Can you name these two QBs? Hints:

The Buccaneer was a former Heisman Trophy winner who had his only good NFL season in 1972 with the 49ers but later made a name for himself as a college coach; the Seahawks starter had four straight solid seasons from 1977 through 1980 and was a regular through 1983.

Perhaps the game's greatest breakaway runner, this Hall of Famer was a constant threat to go all the way before he tore up his knee midway through the 1968 season. He bounced back from surgery to lead the NFL in rushing a year later with 1,032 yards—though his longest gain was a mere 28 yards.

This Heisman Trophy winner's road to success in the NFL was an exceptionally bumpy one. After several years of unfulfilled expectations with the Patriots and the 49ers, he was picked up by the Raiders as a rehabilitation project and threw only 15 passes in two seasons. But he took over as the starting quarterback in 1980 and led them to two Super Bowl victories in the next four seasons. Do you remember this former Stanford star?

In 1966 CBS was the NFL's network, and NBC carried AFL games. Which network televised the first Super Bowl at the conclusion of that season?

On December 20, 1980, in Miami, the Jets beat the Dolphins 24–17 in a Saturday-afternoon game that closed out the season for both teams. It was an undistinguished game except for a unique TV experiment that was conducted that day by NBC. What was the experiment?

In his first 10 seasons, through 1992, this contemporary quarterback threw 158 TD passes and 157 interceptions. In five seasons since then he's thrown for 120 TDs with only 59 interceptions while posting the five highest passer ratings of his career. Who is this surefire Hall of Famer?

Though many consider him a flop as a pro, this Heisman Trophy winner has rushed for more than 8,000 yards (with a high of 1,514 in 1988) and caught more than 500 passes (with a high of 76 in 1986). With the added clue that those are just his NFL totals, can you name him?

 An unheralded 12th-round draft pick in 1967 out of Illinois, this running back lasted 14 years in the NFL and played in five Super Bowls with three different teams. He was on the losing side with the Colts in Super Bowl III and with Dallas in X and XIII, but on the winning side with Pittsburgh in Super Bowl IX and with Dallas in XII. A fine runner for the first half of his career, in his later years he was better known as a reliable third-down receiver out of the backfield.

 In the space of five years, this linebacker from Louisville went from the pinnacle to the pits. As a rookie in 1972, he was a reserve on the Dolphins' undefeated Super Bowl championship team. After three more years in Miami, he moved on to Detroit in 1975 but was taken by Tampa Bay in the expansion draft a year later and suffered through the Buccaneers' 0–14 inaugural season. He returned to the Dolphins for two more years before calling it quits, and he remains the only player to have experienced a season without a loss and a season without a victory.

 This offensive lineman from Dayton was one of the most-traveled players in pro football history. He broke in with the Bengals in 1969 and moved on to Buffalo in 1971. He dropped out of sight for a couple of years, then resurfaced in 1974 with the WFL's Detroit Wheels. When the WFL folded in 1975, he was picked up by the Kansas City Chiefs to finish out the season. He went north to the Canadian Football League in 1976 and stayed through 1980, playing with Hamilton and Edmonton. Again he disappeared for a spell before returning in 1983 with the USFL's L.A. Express. Thus he's the only man to play in four different major leagues—AFL, NFL, WFL, and USFL—not to mention the CFL. If the Hall of Fame had a special wing for perseverance, he'd be a charter member.

This quarterback from Wake Forest began his NFL travels in 1961 with the Redskins. He threw for a total of 5,969 yards in 1962 and '63 with Washington; he amassed 3,399 yards and 29 touchdowns with the Eagles in 1967; after a year as a backup with the Vikings, he led the NFC in passing with the Giants in 1972. Later he spent two years with the 49ers before returning to New York, where he finished his career as a backup for the Giants in 1976. Along the way he passed for 196 touchdowns and more than 30,000 yards.

This kicker broke into the NFL in 1945 with the Eagles, moving on to the Steelers in midseason. He went to the West Coast for two seasons with the L.A. Dons, for whom he led the AAFC in field goals in 1948. He joined the Giants for the 1949 season, then dropped out of sight until returning to the Rams in 1953. Continuing his coast-to-coast act, he rejoined the Giants and stayed in New York until Pat Summerall replaced him in 1958. Two years later, now 41 years old, he resurfaced with the Chargers in the AFL's inaugural season, scoring a career-high 85 points. He hung on through 1964, kicking for four more teams before finally calling it quits. Altogether he scored 655 points in three major leagues, despite a kicking foot that earned him the nickname "The Toeless Wonder."

Game 7

1st Quarter

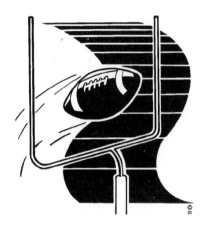

Teams

1. At the time of the merger in 1970, the NFL had 16 teams and the AFL had only 10. When the new 26-team league was split into two 13-team conferences, what three established NFL teams were moved into the AFC?

2. Two NFL teams of the 1990s were named for real people—one a football man, the other a historical figure. Which teams are they?

3. Though they were original members of the AFL, the Oakland Raiders were added at the last minute, after the NFL put an expansion team in one of the eight cities that were to be included in the new league. What city did Oakland replace?

 In the 1930s, when everyone else in the NFL was using some variation of the single wing, one very successful team stuck with its "old-fashioned" T formation. One extraordinary game in 1940 changed everyone's thinking, and within a few years most pro teams were lining up in the T. What game are we talking about, and what was the team that popularized the "retooled" T formation?

 The transition was completed in 1952, when the NFL's last single-wing team finally switched to the T. If I tell you that Joe Geri and Chuck Ortmann had shared the tailback spot in 1951, can you tell me what team it was? For extra credit, can you name the T quarterback, later a very successful general manager, who took over in 1952?

 Perhaps the most famous variation of the single wing appeared in 1937, when a Hall of Fame coach came up with what he called the A formation. His team appeared in the championship game five times in the next 10 years using this formation. Can you name the team and its coach?

 In 1960 the 49ers unveiled the shotgun formation, a return to the days of the single-wing offense. Using it in conjunction with the standard T formation, they finished just a game short of the Western Division title. So, in 1961 the 'Niners went to the shotgun full-time and roared to a 4–1 start before the rest of the league figured out how to stop it. Who was the coach who lived—and died—with the shotgun?

 In making the change to the shotgun, which required a mobile quarterback, the 49ers sent their incumbent QB to the Giants, where he burned up the league for the next three seasons. Give yourself full credit if you can name him and his main replacement, who was beginning a fine career in his own right. For extra credit, can you name the two other signal callers who got significant playing time with the 49ers in 1961? Both of them did more running than passing, but one of them later became a Pro Bowl quarterback himself.

 After 1961 the shotgun formation vanished for more than a decade, until it was revived for use on third-and-long by one of the game's most innovative coaches. Before long, most teams were using it on passing downs. What team made the shotgun part of the modern game, and who was its Hall of Fame coach?

 The profusion of 1,000-yard rushers in the early 1970s sent coaches back to the drawing board in search of a better defense against the running game. And in 1974 the 3–4 alignment made its full-time debut—in the game plan of what AFC team? Again, take an extra bow if you can name its rookie head coach.

 What team of the 1980s developed the attack-mode "46" defense and rode it to a victory in the Super Bowl? And who was the team's defensive coordinator?

 A decade earlier, another Super Bowl winner used a formation known as the "53 defense," so-called because it varied depending on where a certain defender, who wore number 53, lined up. What was the team, and who was the linebacker/defensive end who gave the formation its name?

 The record for fewest points allowed in a 14-game season was set in 1977 by a team that got little recognition for it, probably because it finished with a 7–7 record despite allowing only 129 points. What was the team, and who was its defense-minded head coach?

14 The development of the T formation in the late 1940s created the need for a new, more flexible defense to combat it. And in 1950 the 4–3–4, or "umbrella" defense, appeared. What team created this alignment, which became the standard all over the NFL for more than two decades? And for extra credit, who was the head coach who came up with the idea, and the defensive back (later a pretty fair coach himself) who helped him implement it?

Game 7

2nd Quarter

Minor Leagues and Others

 This QB's NFL career consisted of a single game with the Eagles in 1962. A year later, though, with the Harrisburg Capitols, he was the Atlantic Coast League's MVP, and he was a three-time Continental League MVP with the Orlando Panthers, whom he led to consecutive championships. After the CoFL's demise he went to Canada, where he picked up his fifth MVP Award in 1971 with Winnipeg. From 1963 through 1974 he passed for more than 32,000 yards and 269 touchdowns; often doubling as a kicker, this Penn State alumnus also scored more than 900 points.

 The last independent team that could beat NFL teams on a regular basis was at its peak from 1936 through 1938, its first three years of existence. In '36 and '38 this team played 11 games against NFL clubs, winning 5, losing 3, and tying 3. The 1937 squad may have been its best, but that year the team joined the outlaw AFL and wasn't allowed to play against the established league, so it had to be content with an undefeated season. Can you name this forgotten team?

After three years with the Charleston Rockets of the Continental League, this fine defensive end (and sometimes tackle) caught on with the Rams in 1968 and began a 14-year NFL career with four different teams. An outstanding pass rusher, he was an all-CoFL selection in 1966 and an all-pro in 1972 (with the Rams) and 1976 (with Cincinnati). He was last seen with the Redskins in 1981.

Tim Mara, owner of the New York Giants, created pro football's first true "farm team" in 1938 when he bought a franchise in the American Association. The Jersey City Giants were an instant success, winning the championship, and their biggest star was their Hall of Fame fullback, who booted the astounding total of 13 field goals in an eight-game season. A former New York star who had jumped to the rival AFL in 1936, he rejoined the parent club in 1939 and was still kicking for the Giants as late as 1947.

In a six-year career from 1964 through 1969, most of it with the Charleston Rockets, this punter led his league (the United Football League or the CoFL) four times and compiled a terrific average of 44.2 yards per kick. NFL teams reportedly ignored him because he was slow getting his kicks off, and they may have been right—he did have five blocked in 1969.

After rushing for 327 yards for the Giants in 1966, this back was cut early in the 1967 season and caught on with the Westchester Bulls of the Atlantic Coast League. The Packers picked him up after injuries decimated their backfield, and he made a useful contribution to their championship drive, scoring a touchdown in a first-round playoff against the Rams and making three key gains in the game-winning drive in the Ice Bowl, only a few weeks after his last game in the ACFL. Who was this Yale alumnus?

 The San Diego Bombers won the Pacific Coast Football League championship in 1942, '43, and '44, led by a Notre Dame back whose receiving and breakaway runs made him the most exciting player on the coast. Moving across the country to Washington in 1945, he was a major catalyst as the Redskins earned a trip to the NFL title game. He was almost as good in 1946, but a severely broken leg in the 1947 opener finished him, although he managed to return for a swan song in 1948.

 Playing for the St. Louis Gunners in 1939, this tailback from Tulsa threw for eight touchdowns, third-most in the AFL. Nine years later, now with the Eagles, he led the NFL in passing as his team captured its first championship. When he retired after the 1950 season, his 10,385 career passing yards trailed only Baugh, Luckman, and Graham. Who was he?

 After an all-league season with the Norfolk Neptunes of the Atlantic Coast League in 1971, this defensive lineman with no college experience caught on with the Raiders in 1972 and stuck around through 1978. Who was this two-time all-pro?

 After starring at Fordham, where he was one of the Seven Blocks of Granite, this 190-pound guard was a mainstay of the independent Wilmington Clippers in 1937. The following year he started nearly every game with the Brooklyn Eagles of the American Association. Twenty-two years later, now in his second year as an NFL head coach, he lost to the Eagles in the title game. It was his first and last playoff loss, but far from his last playoff appearance.

 After unsuccessful trials in the Canadian League and with Buffalo of the AFL, this quarterback from Duke joined the Cleveland Bulldogs in 1961 and was named MVP in the United Football League's inaugural season. The team moved to Canton in 1964, and he repeated as MVP, this time leading the Bulldogs to the UFL title. In 1965 the Bulldogs moved to Philadelphia for the Continental League's first season, and our man passed for 33 touchdowns and picked up his third MVP Award (in three different cities, but with the same team). He failed to repeat as MVP in 1966 but closed out his career by throwing 39 TD passes and leading Philadelphia to the championship.

Drafted by the Bears in 1936, this guard from Villanova moved to the Redskins in 1937 and played in every game as the 'Skins won their first championship. Later he was a regular starter for the Eagles for four seasons. But he may have had his best years with the Wilmington Clippers in the American Association, where he was a first-team all-star in 1939, '40, '41, and '47. In 1948 he jumped to Ottawa in what was to become the Canadian League's Eastern Division and added two more all-star seasons to his résumé before calling it quits after the 1950 season.

This 5'11", 165-pound wide receiver played his college ball at little West Liberty State. From 1962 through 1969, with Wheeling, Fort Wayne, and Orlando in the UFL and CoFL, he caught 455 passes for more than 8,500 yards and 93 touchdowns, and played on four championship teams.

A head coach making his debut in the professional ranks led the San Jose Apaches to an 8–4 record and a second-place finish in the Continental League's Pacific Division in 1967. Twenty-two years later he stepped down as an NFL coach after winning his third Super Bowl. Who is this offensive trendsetter?

After a fine career with the Giants from 1934 through 1939, this former NFL passing leader joined the team's Jersey City farm club in 1940 and led the "Little Giants" to the American Association championship. In the process, he completed 62.4 percent of his passes to set a minor league record.

Game 7

3rd Quarter

Get Your Kicks

 This 49er is best known for making 234 consecutive extra points; altogether, he missed only 2 in an 11-year career that ended in 1969. But he really shone as a punter, and his career average of 44.7 yards is the second best ever. Who was this LSU alumnus?

 He's in the Hall of Fame mainly as a defensive back, but this Lions star was also a great punter. He led the NFL three times, with season averages of 48.9, 48.4, and 47.1 yards, and has the third-highest career average, 44.3. He was a five-time all-pro from 1956 through 1962, and in those days they didn't include punters on all-pro squads; if they had, you can bet he would have been chosen a couple more times.

What outstanding kicker set a record in 1967 by making seven field goals in a 28–14 win over the Steelers? From 1963 through 1978 he scored 1,380 points, all for the Cardinals.

That record was matched in 1989 when a former Bronco made seven field goals for Minnesota in an overtime win against the Rams. He kicked a league-high 31 field goals that year, but the Vikings let him go before the next season. Who is this barefoot kicker?

Seven years later, a Dallas kicker accounted for all of his team's points with seven field goals in a 21–6 win over the Packers. Like our last man, he wound up with a different team a year later.

The Broncos had the AFL's leading punter five times in a six-year stretch from 1962 through 1967, but this accomplishment was actually the work of two men. One was a linebacker from Wisconsin who led three years in a row before moving on to Kansas City; the other was a wide receiver from Notre Dame who had two league-leading seasons. The air in Denver probably had something to do with their success, because neither was impressive with other teams. Give yourself full credit if you can name either one.

In 1953 this Hall of Famer made good on 23 of 26 field goal attempts. All the other kickers in the NFL that season combined to make only 85 of 206 kicks, so you can see why our man really stood out from the crowd. Even without any more information, this one should be pretty easy.

The NFL's scoring leader in 1986, he holds an esoteric record for most points in a season or a career scored by a barefoot kicker. A member of the losing team in the Super Bowl with the Eagles and the Patriots, he scored 872 points in a 10-year career that ended with Miami in 1988.

9. This contemporary punter is known for his unusual kicking style, in which his left (nonkicking) foot barely leaves the ground. He led the NFL in punting once, with a 45.7 average in 1991, and he's averaged better than 44 yards in five other seasons. Twice a consensus all-pro, he spent the 1997 season with his fourth different team. Who is he?

10. In 1995, in his first season with a new team, this great kicker booted a record eight field goals of 50 yards or more. Who is this seven-time all-pro? Hint: In 1998 he should become the second-leading scorer of all time.

11. This great punter's average never slipped under 41 yards until his 15th year with the Chiefs, in 1977. He retired a year later with a career average of 43 yards on the nose, after spending his final season with the Patriots. Who is this four-time punting leader?

12. In 1973 this Rams kicker led the NFL with 130 points and 30 field goals. It was his fourth full season, and that gave him a career total of 445 points. But he tallied only 52 more after the goalposts were moved to the back of the end zone a year later, making only 9 of 16 field goals and missing six extra points, and was out of a job in 1975. Who is this Alabama alumnus?

13. In a five-year career this punter from Texas A&M had an undistinguished 40.7-yard average, but as a rookie with the Jets in 1969 he got off the single best punt of all time, a 98-yarder against the Broncos—in Denver, of course. (Though technically a 99-yarder might seem better, actually it would mean a "net" punt of only 79 yards because of the resulting touchback.) He was last seen with the Saints in 1973.

14. A teammate of the last man for a time, this kicker retired after the 1979 season as the second-leading career scorer. In his two best seasons, 1968 and '69, he scored 274 points and booted 66

field goals, leading the AFL in both categories each year. His three field goals provided the winning margin for the Jets in Super Bowl III, and he reached the Super Bowl again nine years later with the Broncos, albeit in a losing cause. Who is he?

 Do you remember the Atlanta Falcon who set a record by punting more than 100 times each season from 1976 through 1978? A three-time all-pro, he finished his 13-year career with the Oilers in 1984.

Game 7

4th
Quarter

Breaking In

1. A rookie wide receiver got the Saints off to a good start in the NFL when he returned the opening kickoff of their first game for a touchdown. The Saints lost that game, however, and had to wait 20 years for their first winning season. The rookie had better luck, becoming a three-time all-pro selection and playing in a Super Bowl with the Vikings before returning to New Orleans for his final season in 1977. Who is he?

2. This Florida Gator started his NFL career with a bang, rushing for more than 1,000 yards in each of his first two seasons. But he missed half of the 1996 season after an extended holdout and lost his job the next year to another flashy rookie,

Warrick Dunn. Our man is now trying to resuscitate his career in Baltimore.

 Joining the Giants as an undrafted rookie in 1943, this Georgia Tech product led the NFL in rushing in each of his first two seasons. He spent most of 1945 in the service, though, and never regained his form afterward. He finished as a part-timer with the Boston Yanks in 1948.

 Some football people used to say it takes a quarterback five years to get himself established, but this 1983 BYU All-American pushed that theory to its limit. After two undistinguished seasons in the USFL, he spent two more frustrating years in Tampa Bay, then four more as a backup to a surefire Hall of Famer. Finally getting a chance as a starter in 1991, he made the most of it, leading the NFL in passing six times in the next seven years.

 Another great quarterback waited in the wings for four years until inheriting the Eagles' starting job in 1961 after Norm Van Brocklin's retirement. All he did was pass for a record 3,723 yards and 32 touchdowns, and he followed that up by leading the NFL in passing yardage four more times in the '60s. In a way, though, the joke was on the Eagles; they traded him after the 1963 season. Who is this pass master from Duke?

 This Clemson grad lived up to his All-American clippings when he broke in with Brooklyn in 1940. He rushed for 411 yards, averaging 6.3 per carry, caught two touchdown passes, and completed three passes for 103 yards and another score to help the Dodgers to a second-place finish, their best ever. But he went into the service after that and never played in the NFL again.

 The NFL's Rookie of the Year in 1969, this Cowboys running back was slowed by injuries for the next two years but rebounded with back-to-back 1,000-yard seasons in 1972 and '73.

Jumping to the WFL in 1975, he suffered a knee injury, and when he returned to the NFL he wasn't the same player. Still, he hung on as a useful third-down back until 1981, first with the Redskins and then with the Browns. Today he's known mainly as the father of an NBA superstar. Who is this star who played his college ball at Yale?

A first-round pick of the Rams in 1996, he broke in by catching 54 passes, 9 for touchdowns, and also returning two punts for scores. His sophomore year was a flop, though, as he failed to score even a single TD. At this point it's anyone's guess whether he'll regain his rookie form. Who is this LSU alumnus?

Another LSU All-American joined the Chicago Cardinals in 1937 and led the league in receiving yardage, beating out Don Hutson. A year later he topped Hutson in receptions. But he sat out the 1939 season in a salary dispute, and when he returned in 1940 he had lost a step. A knee injury that season finished a career that might have been one of the greatest.

A teammate of the last man at LSU, this tailback moved to Chicago with him in 1937 and passed for 804 yards, third best in the league, including the NFL's first recognized 300-yard game against the Bears in the season finale. But he disappeared a year later, after throwing only 39 passes in his sophomore season.

The 1966 AFL Rookie of the Year was a Buffalo running back who rushed for 766 yards and caught 34 passes. He tore up his knee a year later, though, and was finished by 1969, having added only 105 yards to his rookie rushing total. Who was this former Arkansas Razorback?

This two-time All-American from SMU joined the Brooklyn Dodgers in 1936 and finished among the NFL leaders with 505

yards rushing and an average of 4.9 per carry. But having proved that a 5'9", 147-pound back could excel with the big boys, he walked away after that one stellar season.

 The Packers' first-round choice in 1971, this Ohio State running back topped 1,000 yards in each of his first three seasons. But he faded badly after that and bowed out as a backup with the Chiefs in 1977.

 When Sammy Baugh was injured in the first game of the 1938 season, this rookie tailback from Georgia stepped in and kept the Redskins in contention, completing 49 percent of his passes (quite good for that era) and rushing for 195 yards. But the midseason acquisition of Frank Filchock made him the odd man out in the 'Skins' plans, and he left for good after that fine debut.

 Drafted in the 15th round in 1954, this end from little North Alabama made the Bears look like geniuses when he made the all-pro team in his first three seasons. In that span he caught passes for 32 TDs and more than 3,000 yards, averaging well over 20 yards per catch. Injuries slowed him after that, and he was essentially through after 1959, though he hung on until 1962 as a shadow of his younger self.

 The AFL's Rookie of the Year in 1968 was a Bengals back who led the league with 1,023 yards rushing. He never approached that figure again in five more seasons and was last seen with Birmingham of the World Football League in 1974. Who was he?

 In 1969 another Bengal, this one from the University of Cincinnati, led the AFL in passing and gave them a second straight Rookie of the Year. But a shoulder injury short-circuited his career, and he retired after the 1973 season, having thrown only three passes since that great beginning.

Game 8

1st Quarter

World Football League

 The WFL made most of its headlines by signing a few NFL stars. The league's biggest coup came when the Memphis Southmen signed three standouts from the Miami Dolphins for the 1975 season. Who are they?

 The league earned headlines of a negative variety early in the 1974 season when one team admitted that the reported attendance of 120,000 for its first two home games had included about 100,000 freebies and only 20,000 customers who actually paid their way in. What team made the embarrassing revelation?

Perhaps the best-known player who got his start in the WFL was a quarterback and punter with Memphis in 1974 and '75 who went on to lead a team that lost the NFC championship game three years in a row in the early 1980s. Even without the team's name, you should know him.

The Rams made it to the NFC championship game twice in the 1970s with this former WFL quarterback at the helm. Who is the former USC star who made his professional debut in 1975 with the Southern California Sun?

The New York Stars moved to Charlotte during the 1974 season after failing to draw even decent crowds in the nation's largest city, but they did feature two all-WFL defensive linemen who had starred for the Jets' Super Bowl team six years earlier. Finding life in the WFL a far cry from their halcyon days in the Big Apple, they both called it quits after that season. If I tell you that each of them was a three-time all-pro, one at tackle and one at end, can you name them?

The Birmingham Americans had an all-WFL wideout in 1974 who led the league with 1,326 receiving yards. Seven years later, with Atlanta, he led the NFL with 1,358 yards. Altogether he caught 360 passes in nine NFL seasons, all with the Falcons. Who was this diminutive star?

The other two top receivers of the WFL's first season did almost nothing else in the professional ranks. One, a San Diego State alumnus who caught 89 passes for 1,232 yards with the Hawaiians, never played a down in the NFL. The other, a veteran of a single season with the Bengals, led the WFL with 19 touchdown receptions for Memphis. That earned him a second shot in the NFL, this time with the Giants, but after two seasons as a backup he was never seen again. Give yourself full credit if you know either one of them.

The Chicago Winds signed this wideout away from the Vikings for the 1975 season, and he was leading the team in receiving when the franchise went belly-up after five games. Since the WFL season started in midsummer, our man was able to rejoin the Vikings in time for the start of the NFL season. He caught 50 passes and earned the last of his four straight trips to the Pro Bowl. Earlier a star with the Cardinals, he was last seen with the Saints in 1977.

The WFL made touchdowns worth seven points and did away with the traditional conversion attempt by kicking. Instead, teams had to run or pass to tack on an eighth point, which was known by what name?

The league's all-star running backs in 1974 were two rookies who had little success thereafter. The top man, who gained 1,576 yards for the Florida Blazers, averaged less than 2 yards per carry with Jacksonville in 1975 and an even 3 yards per carry in his only NFL season, with Kansas City in 1976. His counterpart, a Rutgers alumnus who picked up 1,524 yards for Memphis, managed only 345 yards with the Philadelphia Bell a year later and never played a down in the NFL. Again, take full credit if you can name one of them.

This defensive tackle from San Jose State played his first two seasons in pro football with the Southern California Sun. After the WFL folded, he put in five solid years with the Chargers and five more with the Rams before bowing out after the 1986 season.

As a rookie with the Jacksonville Sharks in 1974, this tight end from Iowa State caught only six passes. Five years later he was an all-pro selection with the Eagles. A starter with Philadelphia from 1977 through 1981, he was last seen briefly with the Falcons in 1982.

The Chicago Fire's two leading receivers in 1974 both went on to respectable NFL careers. One was a Wake Forest alumnus who had started his professional career with the Pottstown (Pennsylvania) Firebirds of the Atlantic Coast League. His WFL performance earned him a shot with the Broncos, and he gave them four decent seasons as a third wide receiver. The other man joined the Bears in 1976 and caught 175 passes for them from 1976 through 1980. He went to Canada in 1981 and led the Eastern Division in receiving with Montreal; returning to the Bears in 1982, he had little left and called it quits after a single game in 1983. As before, give yourself full credit if you can name either of them.

In 1975 the Jacksonville Express had a rookie defensive back from Tulane who went on to play 11 solid seasons with the Broncos. He intercepted 44 passes in his WFL career and was Denver's starting safety in two Super Bowls. Who was he?

This rookie wide receiver from Iowa State caught 53 passes for the Southern California Sun in 1974, then caught 211 more in the NFL from 1975 through 1981, with a high of 52 in 1976 with the Cardinals. He also had a couple of good seasons with the Saints. Do you remember him?

This quarterback from Purdue played little in the WFL—with New York in 1974 and Chicago in 1975. Catching on with the Lions, he won the starting job in 1978, but injuries sidelined him for much of the next six years. (Still, he threw for more than 3,000 yards in 1980 and 1984.) Moving to the Browns in 1985, he was hurt again and lost the starting job to rookie Bernie Kosar. Sidelined for the whole 1986 season, he returned to back up Kosar for two more years and called it quits after the 1988 season. Who is this luckless QB?

What rookie defensive back with the Chicago Fire in 1974 went on to play eight years with the Oilers, including one appearance in the Pro Bowl and two in the AFC championship game? A Colorado State alumnus, he played his final season with the Saints in 1983.

 This All-American from USC signed with the Southern California Sun in 1975 and didn't disappoint, rushing for 1,200 yards and 16 touchdowns in an abbreviated 12-game season. He was a bust in the NFL, though, gaining only 297 yards for Tampa Bay in 1977 and bowing out after short trials with the Oilers and the Rams a year later.

Game 8

2nd Quarter

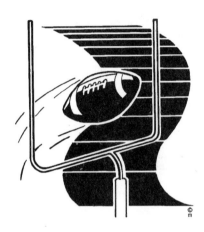

Notorious

 Perhaps the biggest play in the Jets' 16–7 win over the Colts in Super Bowl III came shortly before halftime, when the Colts' quarterback failed to spot a wide-open receiver and missed a game-tying touchdown. Who was the open man, and who was the quarterback who threw elsewhere and had his pass intercepted?

 On September 24, 1950, the Eagles routed the Cardinals 45–7, intercepting eight passes—all of them thrown by the same quarterback, who set a single-game record for passing futility. Two years earlier, with the Rams, he had thrown 114 straight passes without having one picked off. And a week after the debacle against the Eagles, he bounced back with six touchdown passes as the Cardinals clobbered Baltimore. Who is this resilient USC alumnus?

 What quarterback knocked himself out of a nationally televised 1997 game when he made the embarrassing mistake of head-butting the end zone wall after scoring a first-half touchdown?

 With one game to go in the 1978 season, the 11–4 Patriots were gearing up for the playoffs after clinching the AFC East title when their coach made the shocking announcement that he was quitting to take a college post. The demoralized team lost the season finale by 20 points and dropped its first play-off game two weeks later by 17. Who is the coach who let the Patriots down?

 The Dolphins' 27–24 victory over the Chiefs in a 1971 playoff game was only the second to require a second overtime period. It wouldn't have required overtime at all, though, if a Hall of Fame kicker hadn't missed a short field-goal attempt with less than a minute left in the fourth quarter. I won't tell you which team he played for, but you should be able to get him anyway.

 Holding a comfortable 14–0 lead in the fourth quarter of Super Bowl VII, the Dolphins let the Redskins back into the game when their kicker picked up a blocked field goal attempt and tried to throw a desperation pass. In a play destined to be shown on "football blooper" reels forever, the ball slipped out of his hand and was snatched by a Washington defensive back who ran it in for a touchdown. Who was the kicker in question? For extra credit, who was the Redskin who made him pay for his mistake?

 Though he's well known for his scrambling ability, this quarterback was sacked a record 72 times in 1986—and he threw only 209 passes! The team's other two quarterbacks were about as mobile as a couple of tree stumps, but they were sacked 32 times while throwing 303 passes. I'm not going to tell you the team, but can you tell me the name of the often-sacked scrambler? Hint: He had four other seasons in which he was sacked more often than any other quarterback.

A year earlier, another quarterback suffered 62 sacks, setting a record that lasted only a year. But when he wasn't getting dumped, he threw the ball well enough to lead the NFL in passing. He led his team to an 11–5 record and an appearance in the AFC wild-card game, where it lost—and the QB was sacked five more times.

In the second game of 1978, San Diego lost a 21–20 heartbreaker by surrendering a touchdown on the game's final play. What bothered the Chargers was the way it happened: Hit in the backfield, the quarterback tossed the ball forward before he went down, a running back clumsily dribbled it toward the goal line, and the tight end kicked the "fumble" into the end zone before falling on it for a touchdown. The "Holy Roller" play resulted in a rule against forward fumbles in the closing minutes of each half. What team achieved this questionable victory? And who were the three players who helped to rewrite the rule book?

The Rams' first choice in the 1996 draft was released outright during the 1997 season, though he was their leading rusher. Apparently the Rams decided 3.5 yards per carry didn't compensate for a list of off-the-field problems that went back to his college days at Nebraska. Although he was immediately signed by another NFL team, he was released again during training camp in 1998.

Though Washington fans swore the kick was good, this Auburn rookie's missed field goal with seconds left in the final game of the 1939 season cost the Redskins a 10–9 victory over the Giants and the Eastern Division title. A tackle when he wasn't kicking, he played only one more season and tried only one more field goal—which he made.

 Known as one of the greatest "money players" ever, this Hall of Fame quarterback took his team to three straight championship games in the early '50s, plus a divisional playoff in one of those seasons. The team won three of those four games, despite the fact that the QB managed only one touchdown pass while throwing 12 interceptions.

 Under cover of darkness on a night in March 1984, this team loaded its office equipment onto a fleet of moving vans and took off for a new city, leaving behind its home of three decades. Fans in the city still haven't forgotten the name of the owner who left them high and dry. You'll need his name and the name of the team.

 This controversial 1960s quarterback added to his off-the-field legend when he appeared in a TV commercial wearing—gasp!—panty hose. It created something of a scandal at the time, so '60s fans, at least, should have no trouble remembering who we're talking about.

 Trailing 14–12 with less than a minute remaining in a 1980 playoff game, the Browns had the ball on the Raiders' 13-yard line. Before going for a field goal that could have won the game, the Browns took a shot into the end zone, but it backfired when the pass was picked off by Mike Davis, clinching an Oakland victory. Who was the Cleveland quarterback who threw the errant pass? Hint: He was coming off his finest season, having thrown 30 touchdown passes and only 14 interceptions.

Game 8

3rd Quarter

North of the Border

1. A Rose Bowl hero with the Washington Huskies, this quarterback started his professional career in Canada, leading the Edmonton Eskimos to five straight Grey Cup titles. Lured back to the States in a bidding war in 1984, he proved he'd belonged in the NFL all along, starring for more than a decade.

2. This running back from Pitt was a versatile performer for the Browns during their four-year run as champions of the AAFC. In 1950 he jumped to the Hamilton Tiger-Cats and led Canada's Eastern teams in scoring with a record 108 points.

Playing for the Montreal Alouettes from 1952 through 1960, this quarterback from Denver University rewrote the Canadian record book and was a six-time all-star. The Cardinals, led by former CFL coach Pop Ivy, lured him back to the States in 1961, but he developed a sore arm and lost the starting job a year later to Charley Johnson.

 One of the finest linemen of his era, this Tennessee alumnus was an all-pro selection in each of his four years with the Rams, starting in 1947. Jumping to Canada in 1951, he earned all-Western honors four times with Winnipeg and twice more with Calgary; twice, in fact, he was an all-star on offense and defense in the same season. Do you remember him?

 After four seasons in the NFL spent mostly as a backup, this Heisman Trophy winner went north, where he became arguably the greatest quarterback in CFL history, lining his trophy case with Grey Cups and MVP Awards. But he gave it all up in 1998 to try his luck again in the NFL.

 Another Heisman Trophy winner who thrived north of the border was this Oklahoma star who won the Canadian MVP Award in 1953 with the Edmonton Eskimos. Signed by the Colts in 1956, he turned in a decent season but never played again.

 Possibly the most exciting back of the mid-'70s, this Cardinals star shone as a runner, a receiver, and a kick returner. He also tended to fumble a lot—56 times in his prime years, 1973–'77—but that was about the only negative aspect of his style. In 1978 he jumped to Toronto in the CFL, where he starred for three years before returning to the NFL to finish his career with the Redskins in 1981.

 The WFL's passing leader in 1974 with the Southern California Sun, this Utah State alumnus signed with the Chiefs in 1975 and spent the next four years as a backup and occasional starter.

Jumping to Canada in 1979 with the Toronto Argonauts, he led the CFL's Eastern Division in passing but lost his starting job a year later. He resurfaced briefly in 1987 as the Vikings' quarterback in their three "replacement" games. Who is he?

 The Browns' second-leading rusher in 1951 and '52, this Oregon State alumnus went north in 1954 and starred with the Saskatchewan Roughriders for the next six years. A two-time Western all-star as a running back, he was also selected in 1958 as a tight end. That was the position he played when he returned to the United States with the Broncos midway through the AFL's inaugural season. He caught 29 passes in only six games with Denver, then hung up his cleats.

 This running back with no college experience starred with five different Canadian teams from 1954 through 1961 before the Bills signed him in 1962. He was a force to be reckoned with in the AFL, gaining 4,010 yards in his first four seasons and leading the league in rushing twice, before finishing with Denver in 1967.

 Getting a chance to play a bit as Bobby Layne's backup in 1954, this Lion had a fine season and was lured away by the Toronto Argonauts. He made it big in 1955, throwing for 3,561 yards and 30 touchdowns, but never played another full season as a starter, though he hung around for several more years on either side of the border.

 After leading the CFL in punt returns and interceptions in 1979, this three-year Canadian veteran was signed by the Redskins. Used almost solely as a kick returner in the NFL, he was a four-time all-pro in a five-year career, all with Washington. His best season in the States was 1981, when he led the league in kickoff returns and ran two punts back for touchdowns.

The Giants lost an outstanding two-way tackle when this former all-pro jumped to Canada in 1953. Up north he continued his fine play as an all-star on offense and defense three years in a row with the Montreal Alouettes. Who was this former Army All-American?

 An accumulation of injuries forced this star quarterback to retire in 1950 after four seasons in the AAFC. A year later, though, a $25,000 offer persuaded him to try a comeback with the Saskatchewan Roughriders. He lived up to expectations by throwing 28 touchdown passes and leading all punters, and was named the MVP of Western Canada. He reinjured his knee in 1952 but hung on for three more seasons before calling it quits again. Who was this ex-Tulsa star?

 Another AAFC veteran who found happiness in Saskatchewan was this tackle, an all-pro with the Brooklyn Dodgers in 1946 and '47. He entered the NFL in 1950 with the New York Yanks but went north in 1951 to join the Roughriders, for whom he made the Western all-star team four times in the next six seasons— three times as a simultaneous selection on offense and defense. If I add that he played his college ball at Texas A&M, can you name him?

Game 8

4th Quarter

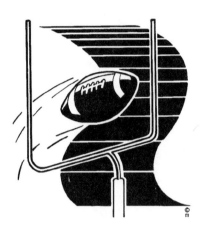

Time Line

1. What year did the NFL sign its first leaguewide television contract? And who was the commissioner who engineered the deal?

2. For years after that, the league held firm to its policy of blacking out telecasts in the home team's viewing area, for fear that local broadcasts would hurt ticket sales. Eventually Congress passed a law requiring sold-out games to be shown locally. What year were the blackouts lifted?

3. When did the NFL inaugurate its two-division format, with the division winners playing a championship game?

What was the first year in which the NFL had a team on the West Coast? And what was the team?

 Starting with the merger in 1970, four teams from each conference made it into the playoffs: three division winners and one wild card. What year was a second wild card added in each conference?

 And when did each conference add a third wild-card team?

 What was the first season in which each team played the same number of games? Hints: The number was 12, and the Packers won the championship that year.

 What was the first season of ABC's *Monday Night Football*? And what three announcers made up the original crew?

 In the game's early years there were limits on the number of players who could enter the game at one time. Today we have unlimited substitution, which allows for separate offensive and defensive teams, not to mention nickel backs, pass-rushing specialists, and others. This policy has been in effect since what year?

 The first NFL draft was held in what year?

 Speaking of the draft, it was the brainchild of an owner who's now in the Hall of Fame. Who was he, and what team did he own?

 What year was overtime instituted to decide tie games during the regular season?

The NFL's first night game took place in what year? Hint: It was played between two now-defunct teams at a place called Kinsley Park. Another hint: The host team's usual home was called the Cyclodrome.

 What year did the NFL begin using instant replay to help officials on the field? And when was the idea dropped?

 While we're on the subject, what league was the first to use instant replays this way?

 The last scoreless tie in the NFL was played in what season? For extra credit, what two teams were involved?

Game 9

1st Quarter

Hall of Fame

 Who has the highest career passer rating in the playoffs? Not surprisingly, his team went 9–1 in those games.

 Though he intercepted 52 passes in a 13-year career and was a consensus all-pro each year from 1966 through 1970, this Cardinals great is mainly remembered as the pioneer of the safety blitz, and as the man who once picked off a pass while playing with a cast on each arm. Who is he?

 A four-time all-pro in the late 1950s, this versatile halfback was a master of the option pass; in a 12-year career he threw

14 touchdown passes, the most of any nonquarterback since the days of the single wing. In fact, his career passer rating of 92.5 is higher than Joe Montana's. Who is this former USC All-American?

A three-time all-pro in an 11-year career, all with the 49ers, this 6'9", 265-pound offensive tackle was one of the most intimidating players of his era, though he seems a bit underqualified for the Hall of Fame. His size made him a formidable kick blocker, but he may have been best known for his habit of eating raw meat.

What quarterback played in a championship game in each of his 10 seasons? No one else can match that, or even come close.

This former Notre Dame star held the career and single-game records for receptions and yardage in playoff games when he retired after the 1945 season. But though he was a very good two-way end with the Redskins for seven years, he was never named to an all-pro first team during his career. Still, in 1968 the Hall of Fame selectors decided he was worthy of enshrinement. Who was this marginal immortal?

During a fine 13-year career with the Lions and Eagles, this center and linebacker from Fordham was named a first-team all-pro exactly once—in 1944, when *Pro Football Illustrated* included him on its team. But in 1968 he was inducted into the Hall of Fame along with the last man. A college star at Fordham, he broke into the NFL in 1938.

The Browns drafted this lineman from Grambling in the 15th round in 1956 and spent a couple of years trying to decide whether he should play offense or defense. Finally they shipped him to Green Bay, where Vince Lombardi immediately installed him as a full-time defensive end. His 10 years as a Packer included five all-pro seasons and five championships.

This man was named Coach of the Year an incredible nine times, with two different teams. He coached in 11 championship games but none in his last 13 years on the job. Who was he?

 Despite the fuss Jim Brown made over the possibility that this man would break his career rushing record, it didn't happen, and he finished with "only" 12,120 yards and an even 100 touchdowns. On the other hand, he did establish the playoff record for rushing yards, with 1,556, and touchdowns, with 18. The latter mark has been broken, but the former still stands. Last seen with the Seahawks in 1984, he's known for his accomplishments with another team.

 This graceful wide receiver caught 427 passes in his 13-year career, somewhat low for a Hall of Famer in his era (the '60s and '70s). But he certainly made them count, averaging better than 20 yards per reception and hauling in 85 touchdown passes. An eight-time all-pro, he played in seven league or conference championship games, plus three Super Bowls. Who is this Ohio State alumnus?

 This seven-time all-pro was the greatest center of the 1940s, and in the era of two-way football he also excelled on defense. In fact, he led the NFL in interceptions in 1942, making him the only linebacker to do so.

 An all-pro for eight consecutive seasons in the 1960s, this offensive tackle also played on five championship teams during those years. No less an authority than Vince Lombardi called him "the finest player I ever coached." Later, serving as a head coach himself, he took an underdog Bengals team to the Super Bowl. Who is he?

 Who was the first Hall of Fame quarterback to play for the Baltimore Colts?

This linebacker played his whole career with the same team from 1981 through 1992. He was a nine-time all-pro, a three-time selection as defensive Player of the Year, and an easy choice for the Hall of Fame as soon as he became eligible. (If you're thinking of Lawrence Taylor, this isn't he.)

Game 9

2nd Quarter

Nicknames

1. Greasy

2. Hacksaw

3. The Hammer

4. Hollywood

5. Hopalong

6. The Human Bowling Ball

7. Hunk

8. Ice Cube

9. Ickey

10. Ironhead

11. The Jet

12. Jug

13. Juice

14. Kink

15. Little Train

Game 9

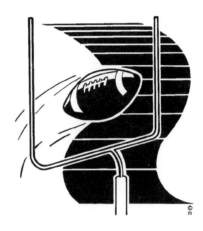

3rd
Quarter

Last Hurrahs

This all-pro receiver caught 94 passes for 18 touchdowns in 1994 but was forced to retire in the off-season for medical reasons. Still, he caught nearly 600 passes in a seven-year career.

He led the league's rushers in 1937, his sixth season, and helped the Redskins to their first championship. It was his second rushing title and his fourth year as a first-team all-pro. But he quit the game for a college coaching job when the team's owner wouldn't raise his $4,000 salary for the following season.

The NFC's third-leading passer in 1993, he led his team to an 11–5 record but was released after the season, ostensibly because of his age (he had just turned 39). The team is still looking for someone to replace him.

 His fifth year with the Packers, 1942, was his best—and also his last. All he did was pass for a league-leading 2,021 yards and 24 touchdowns, setting new marks in both categories.

 This 40-year-old quarterback led the NFC in passing in 1974, his 18th season, then "retired" when George Allen made it clear that he wouldn't be welcomed back.

 He caught 62 passes for the Eagles in 1955. That was enough to lead the NFL for a third straight season, but he retired rather than go for a fourth.

 A neck injury ended this speedy receiver's career after he caught 59 passes for the Bengals in his 1991 finale. He totaled 363 receptions in seven years and had his best season in 1988, when he gained 1,273 yards and averaged 24 yards per catch en route to his only Super Bowl appearance. Do you remember the former Miami Hurricane who was 1985's Rookie of the Year?

 In 1968 this quarterback may have had his best season, ranking second in the NFL in passing and leading the Cowboys to a 12–2 record. He was only 30 years old at the time, but he retired in the off-season. Who is this former SMU star?

 The Cowboys lost another mainstay during that same off-season when their top running back bowed out. He had ranked sixth in rushing in 1968 with 836 yards, which was just about what he averaged in an exceptionally consistent eight-year career that earned him six trips to the Pro Bowl.

The NFL interception leader in 1984, this Seahawks safety was a consensus all-pro each year from 1982 through 1985. Injuries slowed him a bit over the next two seasons, but he was an all-pro selection again in 1987 even though he was forced to retire after the season, still a year short of his 30th birthday. Who is this UCLA product?

Bouncing back from a broken leg, this Hall of Fame quarterback established career highs for completions (345) and yards (3,468) in 1978, his final season, and also threw for 25 touchdowns. On the downside, he also set another career high in interceptions, with 32.

The NFL's first effective 300-pounder, this middle guard (much like a nose tackle of today) was a consensus all-pro with the Lions in 1954, his final season. It was his fourth all-pro season in a row, and he was only 29 when he called it quits. Who was this immovable object?

A consensus all-pro in his final season, 1945, he led the NFL in receptions. But since he finished only second in yardage, TD receptions, and scoring, this actually wasn't one of his best seasons.

His 1988 season with the Cardinals was pretty typical of his career; he passed for 3,395 yards and 20 touchdowns, with only 11 interceptions. But a hip injury forced him out of the game before the next season, and he never played again.

This Dolphins center's final season, 1987, was his fifth straight year as a consensus all-pro, but he went down with a serious knee injury and was never able to play again. Though the injury shortened his career, it didn't keep him from being elected to the Hall of Fame in 1998.

The first Heisman Trophy winner to play in the NFL, he topped the league in passing yardage as a rookie in 1939, then led with 124 completions in his 1940 swan song. And in his final game he riddled the Redskins' secondary for 33 completions in 60 attempts, both record totals at the time. Who was this diminutive TCU tailback?

Yet another Heisman winner bowed out by throwing for 3,586 yards and 27 touchdowns in 1979, both career highs, and leading the NFL in passing for the second straight year. In his final regular-season game, he led his team to a comeback 35–34 win over the Redskins by throwing for two TDs in the game's final minutes.

This Cincinnati cornerback intercepted 65 passes in a 15-year career, including 8 in his 1983 finale, 2 of which he returned for touchdowns. He was also an all-pro selection for the third time. Who is this Bengal who went out with a bang?

Game 9

4th Quarter

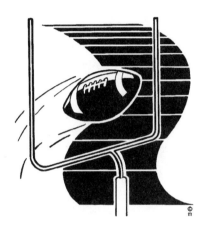

Many Happy Returns

This outstanding return man led the NFL three times in punt return yardage, once in kickoff return yardage, and once in punt return average in a career that lasted from 1964 through 1973. His best years came with the Colts and the Rams, but he also played single seasons with the Eagles, Redskins, and Oilers. Who is he?

In 1979 and '80 this Kansas City speedster returned punts for a total of 1,193 yards and four touchdowns. With the Cardinals in 1986 and '87 he caught a total of 171 passes for 2,131 yards and 14 touchdowns. Last seen with Phoenix in 1990, he finished with 544 receptions in a 13-year career. Can you name him?

A failure as a wide receiver with three different teams, this former Heisman Trophy winner came out of nowhere in 1996 to shatter the record for punt return yards with 875, including three for touchdowns. He kept it up in the playoffs too, returning a punt and a kickoff for TDs and winning the MVP Award in the Super Bowl.

Despite his heroics, the last man still fell one short of the record for punt return touchdowns in the regular season. It was set in 1951 by a Detroit rookie who also averaged 19.1 yards per return. A year later he averaged 21.5 yards but reached the end zone "only" twice. He never duplicated those two seasons, but he led the NFL twice in interceptions and wound up in the Hall of Fame.

The single-season record for punt return touchdowns was tied in 1976 by a Broncos standout who was also the first to amass 3,000 punt return yards. A three-time leader in punt return average, he also became a reliable receiver in the latter part of his career, with a high of 64 receptions in 1979. Who is he?

For years the previous two men shared the record for career punt return touchdowns with eight, but that mark fell in 1997 when this Charger returned three punts for scores, running his total to nine in a nine-year career. It was his first season in San Diego, after stints with two other teams.

The last man was returning kicks for the Chargers because their previous return man, the career leader in punt return average, had signed with Denver in the off-season. And oddly enough, he too returned three punts for touchdowns in 1997. Who is this Stanford alumnus?

The career record for punt return yardage still belongs to this former Oiler and Falcon who piled up 3,317 yards in a 14-year career. A two-time leader in punt return average, he also had some good seasons as a receiver, catching 64 passes for Atlanta in 1983 and 62 more two years later. Despite all that, he might be best remembered for his rubber-legged end-zone dance. You shouldn't need his nickname to get him.

The two highest single-season kickoff return averages were both achieved in 1967. The leader was a Packers rookie whose 41.1 average included four touchdowns, another record. Right behind him was a Hall of Fame running back who averaged 37.7 yards and returned three for touchdowns. Can you name them both?

Speaking of kickoff returns, this former Nebraska Cornhusker had an incredible three-year run with the Saints from 1994 through 1996, with consecutive yardage totals of 1,556, 1,617, and a record 1,791. In his rookie year, 1993, he led the NFL in punt return yardage and average.

In seven years with the 49ers, this star led the NFL three times in kickoff returns and once in punt returns. His career kickoff return average is third best of all time, and he was no slouch as a defensive back, either—a five-time all-pro in a nine-year career, the last two with the Cardinals.

The first to lead his league in punt and kickoff returns in the same season was a Denver rookie who paced the AFL in both categories in 1969, averaging 11.5 yards on punts and 28.5 yards on kickoffs. He was also a fine safety, a four-time all-pro in a 13-year career. Who was this Broncos star?

In his first five seasons, this Packers safety and punt returner averaged 11.3 yards on 91 returns, including a league-leading 16.1 average in 1961. Over the next seven years he returned 96 more punts for a puny 3.8-yard average. His work at safety didn't suffer, though, and he was an all-pro in each of his last 10 years. Who is this Hall of Famer?

As a wide receiver this contemporary standout has caught 599 passes in a 10-year career, but he's also been a standout return man. As a rookie he was the NFL's best kickoff returner, and he's one of only five players with more than 3,000 yards on punt returns. Can you name this former Notre Dame star?

The Falcons plucked this return man from the Bears in the expansion draft, and he responded by leading the NFL in kickoff return yards in 1966 and '67. In 1972, by now back in Chicago, he was the league's top kickoff returner with a 30.8-yard average; a year later, playing for the Chargers, he returned two punts for touchdowns. In a 10-year career with five different teams, he returned kickoffs for a record 6,922 yards (though two players have surpassed that total since). Who is this Wisconsin alumnus?

This 5'8" speedster led the NFL in punt return yardage as a rookie in 1949, then led in kickoff return yardage a year later, with a league-leading 33.7-yard average and three touchdowns. He never matched those two performances in a five-year career, all of it with the Rams. His nickname might give him away, so you'll have to get him without it.

Game 10

1st Quarter

NFL Pioneers

Until Sammy Baugh came along, this Michigan All-American was the greatest passer in the history of football. Forgotten today, he was on every all-pro team from 1927 through 1930, and threw an incredible 20 touchdown passes in 1929 for the Giants. Inexplicably ignored by the Pro Football Hall of Fame, he became very bitter about it and eventually committed suicide in 1982.

This outstanding all-around back from Syracuse was a mainstay of the Giants in their first three seasons of existence, leading the NFL in scoring as they captured their first championship in 1927. He repeated as the scoring leader in 1930 with

Brooklyn and was a consistent passer (31 TD passes) and line plunger. When his playing career was over, he was instrumental in the formation of the AFLs of 1936–37 and 1940–41, coaching New York teams in each league.

Starting out with the New York Yankees of the 1926 AFL (a.k.a. "the Red Grange league") and entering the NFL with the team in 1927, this great guard joined the Packers in 1929, not coincidentally the first of their three straight championship seasons. A seven-time all-pro, he was among the second group of inductees into the Hall of Fame. Who was this Penn State product?

Another great guard of somewhat earlier vintage was this four-time all-pro who earned his first honors with Detroit in 1925 and starred for Providence when the Steam Roller won the 1928 NFL title. At times he also served as a kicker, booting 14 field goals in two years with Detroit. In his day he may have been best known for winning the championship of professional wrestling in 1929. Who was this 5'6", 200-pound fireplug?

Pro football's finest receiver before Don Hutson was this free spirit who played from 1925 through 1938 under a pseudonym inspired by a Rudolf Valentino movie. A member of the first group of Hall of Fame inductees, he caught an amazing 11 touchdown passes in 1931 with the Packers, and as far as we can tell from unofficial statistics, he retired as the career leader in receptions and interceptions. He started his pro career with Milwaukee and finished with Pittsburgh, but enjoyed his best years in Green Bay.

The era of big-time pro football in Ohio that led to the formation of the NFL began in 1915 when the Canton Bulldogs signed the game's greatest player for an astonishing $250 per game. Who was this Hall of Famer?

When the Bulldogs played their archrivals that season, their opponents' lineup included two Notre Dame greats: a quarterback who was one of the top passers in the early pro game, and an end who was his favorite receiver. After starring in college, they both played professionally for several seasons in the pre-NFL era. Can you name them? Hint: The end became perhaps the most famous college coach of all time; the quarterback coached the Lions for five years in the 1940s.

While we're on the subject, who *were* the Bulldogs' archrivals? After sharing the unofficial Ohio League championship with Canton in 1915, they fell short in 1916, '17, and '19, losing key late-season games to them each year. But they did beat Canton once in 1917—the Bulldogs' only loss during their three championship seasons.

A five-time all-pro, this end from Marquette may have been the best player on the Packers' three-time champs of 1929–31. Ignored by the Hall of Fame, he was one of the two finest ends of the pre-Hutson era. And, Hutson replaced him in the Packers' lineup when he retired after the 1934 season.

The greatest dropkicker ever was also a great all-around back from Northwestern who began his professional career in 1917 with a team in Hammond, Indiana, scoring 72 points in 10 games. In the NFL, playing from 1920 through 1929 with the Chicago Cardinals and the Bears, he tallied a record 426 points, leading the league in 1923 and '26. He led four times in field goals and booted a record 51 for his career. Who was he?

This Nebraska alumnus was the best punter of the 1920s, an all-pro halfback from 1926 through 1929, and another mainstay of the Packers' 1929–31 champions. On top of that, he was the first player to score as many as 50 touchdowns. But it wasn't enough to impress the Hall of Fame selectors.

This center from Missouri spent three seasons in the NFL with three different teams and was a first-team all-pro selection each year. He broke in with the Kansas City Cowboys in 1926 and helped them improve to an 8–3 record, good for fourth place in a 22-team league. When that team folded, he caught on with the newly formed Cleveland Bulldogs, who finished fourth in 1927 with an 8–4–1 record. The Bulldogs faded away during the off-season, and our man moved on to the Providence Steam Roller, which surprised everyone by winning the championship in 1928. You've probably never heard of him, but he was one of the best in the NFL's first decade.

In 1922 this NFL original led the league in rushing touchdowns and TD passes. In 1923 he coached Milwaukee to a surprising 7–2–4 record and a fourth-place finish; in 1925 he organized a new team in Detroit and finished third with a record of 8–2–2. As a player-coach with Providence in 1927 he caught more than 30 passes, a very high total for his era; a year later, injured early in the season, he coached from the sidelines as the Steam Roller won the championship. And two decades after that, as coach of the Cardinals, he reached the title game two years in a row, winning in 1947 and losing in '48. Who was this multitalented football great?

Named to the first two "official" all-pro teams, this 190-pound guard from Dartmouth was one of the standout linemen of the 1920s. Known for blocking punts, he played his best seasons with Buffalo's fine teams of the early '20s, but was around as late as 1927 with the Frankford Yellow Jackets and was a key player with Frankford's 1926 champs. His given name was Adolf, but he was universally known by a different moniker.

Game 10

2nd Quarter

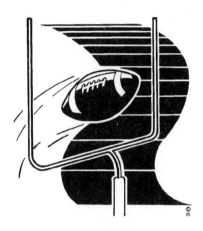

Milestones

Because of the tendency to focus on the number of receptions as the measure of a receiver, few noticed when this former Packers star broke the record for career receiving yards early in the 1992 season. By that time he was with Buffalo, after a brush with the law that hurt his public image, and of course Jerry Rice shattered his record before long. But few could match him for big-play ability.

His 51.4-yard punting average in 1940 is still the best ever, as is his career mark of 45.1. He also set a pair of interception records in 1943, with 11 for the season and 4 in one game. He had less luck with these: the former mark has since been surpassed, and the latter has been tied many times, though never beaten.

A former Tulsa All-American has a higher career punting average than the last man, but he's not in the NFL record books because he played his whole four-year career in the AAFC. He averaged 46.4 yards on 231 kicks, including a 49.1 mark with the Los Angeles Dons in 1948, a year in which he also led the league in completions and gained 2,403 yards through the air. In 1946, playing for Brooklyn, he was the league's MVP.

When he retired after the 1939 season, he was listed as the NFL's career rushing leader. Later research revealed that he wasn't, and anyway all rushing records from those days have been shattered. Still, for eight years he was one of the game's best power runners. Playing at the same time as Nagurski and Hinkle, he rarely made any all-pro teams, but he did play on a championship team with Detroit in 1935. In his best individual season, 1936, he gained 827 yards but missed the last couple of games and saw Tuffy Leemans pass him to win the rushing title by three yards.

Quick, now: What great running back topped the 100-yard mark a record 14 times in 1997—in consecutive games, no less?

On December 12, 1965, a rookie running back broke loose for six touchdowns, including plays of 85, 80, and 50 yards, in a 61–20 demolition of the 49ers, tying the single-game record. Who was this future Hall of Famer?

The first receiver to catch as many as 80 passes in a season, this Hall of Famer snagged 84 in 1950 with the Rams, leading the league for the third year in a row.

That record stood until 1964, when a flanker for the Bears hauled in 93 passes. It was 35 more than the second-highest total in his 10-year career.

The first NFL player to hit the century mark in receptions was this star who caught 106 passes in 1984. It was no fluke; he caught 834 others in his long career.

 However, two receivers managed to reach triple figures in the early years of the AFL. The first man did it for the Broncos in 1961, catching 100 passes right on the nose. Though he never reached triple digits again, he did lead the AFL in receptions in five of the league's first six seasons.

 The lone blot on the previous man's record came in 1964, when this end for the Oilers caught a record 101 passes. He also gained 1,546 yards, but that wasn't a record, because it was 200 yards short of his own 1961 total.

 In 1994 this Viking set a new standard for receivers by catching 122 passes, a total he matched in 1995, and he's currently working on a streak of five straight 1,000-yard seasons. He joined the Vikes in 1990, after his first coach released him, saying, "All he can do is catch touchdowns." Who is this sure-handed star? And who was the coach who let him go?

 The first running back to reach the century mark in receptions, this Cardinals standout caught 101 passes in 1995 and 99 more a year later. Who is this two-time Pro Bowl selection?

 In 1951 a receiver with the Rams caught 66 passes for 1,495 yards and 17 touchdowns, averaging 22.7 yards per catch—all this in a 12-game season. Each of those figures led the league by a considerable margin; his yardage topped the second-best total by more than 600 yards and beat Don Hutson's record by almost 300. The touchdown total tied another of Hutson's records. All things considered, it may be the greatest season any receiver ever had, so good that the rest of our man's outstanding career pales alongside it. Who is this Hall of Famer?

Game 10

3rd Quarter

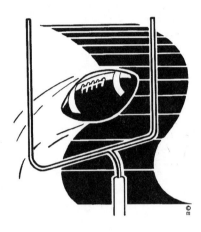

Second Careers

 In 1989 this Raiders back rushed for 950 yards in the fall after racking up 32 home runs and 105 RBIs while pursuing his "hobby" as a major league outfielder over the summer. But a serious hip injury suffered during an NFL playoff game derailed him in both sports after 1990.

 He quarterbacked the Chargers and the Bills to five championship-game appearances in his nine-year career and played in seven AFL all-star games despite career totals of 114 touchdowns and 183 interceptions, the worst ratio ever among QBs with more than 100 of either. Apparently he made up for that weakness with leadership, and it may have been the same quality that later earned him a seat in the House of Representatives and a Cabinet post.

After a 13-year career as a defensive end with the Giants and the Rams, he left the game for an acting career. It proved to be a profitable move, because he soon earned the title role in a long-running cop show.

This Colorado State grad was nicknamed "Tarzan" because he played the ape man in a couple of movies. He saw little action as an end with the Lions in 1940, his only NFL season, and finished the year with the Columbus Bullies, who won the AFL championship. He also played with the minor league Hollywood Stars in 1938, two years after winning the decathlon in the 1936 Olympics.

This elongated defensive end shocked the Cowboys when he retired in 1979 to become a boxer. Though he won all six of his fights, they were all against nobodies, and by 1980 he was ready to play football again. The layoff didn't hurt his career, really; all three of his Pro Bowl appearances came after his return. Who is this would-be pugilist?

This Colorado All-American led the nation in rushing and total offense in 1937 and finished second in the balloting for the Heisman Trophy. He followed that up by leading the NFL in rushing twice in a three-year career with Pittsburgh and Detroit. He was one of the most celebrated players of the '30s, but today he's much better known as a former Supreme Court justice.

The Rams drafted this basketball star from USF in 1955 as a defensive back, despite the fact that he hadn't played any football in college. In training camp, applying the principles of the full-court press, he's said to have invented bump-and-run coverage. The Rams were impressed, but he left to concentrate on

basketball. And it paid off: He picked up several championship rings as a player and coach with the Celtics.

 Another future Celtics great was taken in the seventh round
by the Browns in 1962, though he too hadn't played football
since high school. Fresh out of Ohio State, he played in one
exhibition game with Cleveland before being cut—more for a
lack of experience than a lack of ability. He went on to score
more than 26,000 points in a 16-year NBA career.

 A four-time all-pro with the Raiders, this former defensive end
did a creditable job in a supporting role in a 1996 film called
Broken Arrow. But an attempt to turn him into a leading man in
the 1997 action film *Fire Storm* didn't fare well with the critics
or at the box office.

 He retired after the 1989 season as the NFL's career receiving leader. A few years later he embarked on a new career
as a member of the Oklahoma delegation in the House of
Representatives.

 An All-American from little St. Mary's in California, where he
was noted for his twisting, dodging runs, this native of Hawaii led the AAFC in punt return yardage in 1948 and kickoff
return yardage a year later. Those were his only two seasons in
pro football, but he returned to the public eye a couple of decades later as a television actor, with a regular role on—what
else?—*Hawaii Five-O*.

 In 1963 he batted .147 in 61 games with the Washington Sena-
tors; three years later his interception in the end zone with 28
seconds left clinched the Packers' 34–27 victory in the 1966 NFL
championship game against Dallas, paving the way for Green
Bay's trip to the first Super Bowl.

In 1917, playing under a pseudonym as "Foster," he was a standout end for the Canton Bulldogs, champions of professional football; two years later he batted .357 as an outfielder for the Cincinnati Reds when they won the World Series against the "Black Sox." In the 1940s he coached back-to-back NFL champions, and in 1969 he was inducted into the Pro Football Hall of Fame. Who was this man for all seasons—well, for two seasons, anyway?

 What great running back shocked the football world when he retired before the 1966 season to star in a movie called *The Dirty Dozen?*

Game 10

4th
Quarter

Teammates

Name the all-pro running backs who played beside the following lesser-known backs, some of them pretty talented in their own right:

 Jim Braxton, Buffalo

 Maurice Carthon, New Jersey Generals and New York Giants (either of two)

 Ernie Green, Browns (either of two)

Charlie Harraway, Browns and Redskins (either of two)

 Daryl "Moose" Johnston, Cowboys

 Bosh Pritchard, Eagles

 Tim Wilson, Oilers

 Two quarterbacks from the same team finished first and second among NFL passers in 1951. They're both in the Hall of Fame, so I won't give you their team. Can you name them?

 Charlie Trippi's arrival in 1947 completed the Cardinals' Dream Backfield, which led the team to its only title since 1925. Who were his three famous backfield mates? For real experts, what prewar Cardinals star was relegated to a backup role when Trippi arrived?

 They had no catchy nickname and won no championships, but from 1954 through 1956 the 49ers had an even more illustrious backfield corps, all of whom are now in the Hall of Fame. (In comparison, two members of the Cardinals' Dream Backfield are enshrined at Canton.) Can you name the 49ers' crack quartet?

 The Rams' great defensive line of the 1960s, the Fearsome Foursome, actually included five players, because one member was replaced in 1967. Give yourself full credit if you know four.

Another great defensive front four was the heart of the Vikings' famed defense, the Purple People Eaters. Again, the group includes five players in all, but you need only four.

 Pittsburgh's Steel Curtain defense in the 1970s was built around yet another star-studded defensive line. Can you name them?

 After registering a mere 28 sacks in 1980, the Jets posted an NFL-leading 66 in 1981, and their front four were dubbed the New York Sack Exchange. Who made up this pass-rushing quartet?

 The Giants' front four of the late 1950s and early '60s were the foundation of a team that reached the championship game six times in eight years. And along with middle linebacker Sam Huff, they became one of the first famous defensive units. Do you remember them?

Game 11

1st Quarter

Notorious

 Two of the NFL's top stars missed the 1963 season when they were suspended for betting on games. One was a running back and kicker with the Packers, the other a defensive tackle with the Lions. The tackle starred for several years after the suspension, but the back was never the same.

 Who missed a 47-yard field goal with seconds to go in Super Bowl XXV that would have given the championship to Buffalo? Instead, the Giants escaped with a 20–19 win.

 In 15 years with the Cardinals, this Hall of Famer set standards for tight ends with 480 receptions for 7,918 yards. But in his

16th season, with the Cowboys, he dropped a sure touchdown pass in the Super Bowl against the Steelers. The Cowboys lost 35–31, and for many fans the memory of that one dropped pass wiped out a terrific career. Who was this star-crossed star?

 By popular acclaim, this man holds the dubious honor of being the most vicious hitter in pro football history. A linebacker with seven teams in a 10-year career, he spent his best years with the 49ers in the early 1950s, even making it to the Pro Bowl once, but he was best known for his brutal technique of drilling his shoulder into an opponent's chin—this at a time when many players still had no faceguards on their helmets. Last seen with Denver in the first season of the AFL, he left a trail of broken jaws behind as testimony to his lethal style.

 Trying to improve his team's winning percentage before the end of the 1925 season, owner Chris O'Brien hastily scheduled two games for the second week of December with Milwaukee and Hammond, two teams that had disbanded for the year. Hammond was able to reassemble a competitive squad and dropped a 13–0 decision to O'Brien's team. Milwaukee, though, had trouble filling out its lineup and eventually recruited four high school players who couldn't help them avert a 58–0 debacle. When NFL president Joe Carr found out, he fined O'Brien and ordered the Milwaukee owner to sell his team. As a result of this embarrassment, O'Brien never formally accepted the championship trophy. What was the name of O'Brien's team? Hint: They're still around today, but in a different city.

 OK, now an easy one. This quarterback's career ended during a Monday night game in 1985 when his leg was snapped like a twig on a sack by the Giants' defense. Even casual fans will remember this, since it was probably the most replayed injury in sports history.

 Just a few years later, a Bengals defensive lineman suffered a similar injury when he snapped a bone in his leg while making a tackle in Super Bowl XXIII against the 49ers. Unlike our last man, he resumed his career and played several more seasons.

Frank Gifford sat out the whole 1961 season after being blindsided by what Eagles linebacker in a key late-season game in 1960?

A lot of folks in Baltimore still say their team was robbed in the 1965 Western Division playoff when the officials called this veteran Packers kicker's game-tying field goal good. Green Bay won in sudden death, but diehard Colts fans still say it should have been over in regulation. Hint: The kicker doubled as a punter and had spent the previous nine years with the Giants.

On the Redskins' first possession in the 1940 championship game, a wide-open receiver dropped Sammy Baugh's pass on the 5-yard line for what would have been a game-tying touchdown. It was all downhill for the 'Skins after that, and the final score, as you probably know, was 73–0. (Asked later about how the dropped pass might have changed the game, Baugh replied, "I reckon it would have been 73–6.") The end who muffed that pass had led the Redskins in receptions in 1934, '35, '37, and '38 and retired as the team's career leader. Who was he?

The star of Super Bowl VI was a Dallas back who rushed for 95 yards and a touchdown, but his most memorable performance of the day may have come in a postgame interview. Known for not talking to the media, or even his teammates, he showed up with football legend Jim Brown as his intimidating companion. Brown did most of the talking, while the Dallas star answered mainly in monosyllables. Who was this man of few words? And for true aficionados, who was the interviewer, a former Eagles defensive back, who suffered through a broadcaster's nightmare?

A few years later, a straight-arrow quarterback caused something of a stir on a TV interview when he said (paraphrased), "I enjoy sex; I just enjoy it with my wife." Can you name him? And do you remember the interviewer, who was one of the first women in football broadcasting?

A two-time all-pro, this Raiders defensive lineman of the 1970s didn't play college football. That fact, combined with his eccentric personality, led *Monday Night Football* commentator Alex Karras to say his alma mater was the "University of Mars."

In his first five years with the Browns he rushed for more than 2,500 yards and caught more than 200 passes, but he's remembered in Cleveland for his fumble that cost the Browns a game-tying touchdown in the final minutes of the 1987 AFC championship game. Finally sent packing by the Browns, he bounced back to have a pair of 1,000-yard seasons with the Redskins.

Two members of the New York Giants were barred from the NFL for life for not reporting a bribe offer before their 1946 championship game against the Bears. One, a fullback from Mississippi, never played in the NFL again; the other, a tailback-turned-quarterback, went to Canada and kept after the NFL until he was finally reinstated in 1950. Having made his point, he threw three passes for Baltimore before calling it quits.

Game 11

2nd Quarter

Yesterday's Heroes

1. The Giants' first 1,000-yard rusher turned the trick in 1970, his first year in New York after spending his rookie year with the Browns. He missed most of the 1971 season with a knee injury, then bounced back to gain 1,182 yards in 1972 and 902 a year later. Injuries caught up with him after that, though, and he was finished after the 1975 season. Also a fine receiver out of the backfield, he caught 213 passes in a seven-year career.

2. The NFC reception leader in 1981 and '82, this end from Clemson isn't as well remembered as he might be, largely because his stats pale beside those of Jerry Rice, who succeeded him as Joe Montana's favorite target. Still, he caught 506 passes in a nine-year career, all with the 49ers.

This two-time All-American from Texas was the first player chosen in the 1966 NFL draft. He was also the first player drafted by the Falcons, who joined the league that year. It was his misfortune to spend his whole 11-year career with Atlanta, and also to play the same position as Dick Butkus, who held down the middle linebacker spot on most all-pro teams. Though our man occasionally made an all-pro team and played in five Pro Bowls, injuries and the poor performance of his team cast a shadow over his career. Still, some experts say he, not Butkus, was the best linebacker of his era.

Vince Lombardi gave this Redskins rookie a starting job in 1969, and he responded by rushing for 5,037 yards in his first five seasons. He led the NFL in rushing in 1970 and was the league's MVP in 1972. But his punishing style of play took its toll after that, and he was through after the 1976 season. Do you remember this three-time all-pro?

A nearly unanimous all-pro selection every year from 1958 through 1962, this consummate safety played in six championship games with the Giants. Another who's been inexplicably overlooked by the Hall of Fame, he picked off 52 passes in a 12-year career and also returned two kicks for touchdowns as a rookie. Can you name this forgotten star from Mississippi?

Despite the fact that they're tied for sixth in career interceptions with 62 apiece, these two defensive backs are surprisingly unrecognized. One was an Ohio State product who starred for the Lions in the 1960s, playing in three Pro Bowls; the other played on a Super Bowl winner as a rookie with the Steelers in 1975 but spent the rest of his career with the Seahawks and the Packers, appearing just once in the Pro Bowl. Take full credit if you can name either one of them.

Of all the track stars who have tried to make the transition to football, the most successful was this wide receiver who set a world record and won a gold medal in the 100-meter dash in the 1964 Olympics. From 1965 through 1971 with the Cowboys he caught 67 touchdown passes and averaged better than 20 yards per catch; he also starred as a punt returner, leading the league with a 20.8-yard average in 1968. Who was the three-time all-pro they called "Bullet"?

This Mississippi All-American took over the Giants' quarterback job in 1948 and didn't relinquish it until 1961. The 1948 Rookie of the Year, he was named MVP in 1959 by the NFL players and the Associated Press. A seven-time finalist in the Hall of Fame balloting, he never made the final cut, but when he retired after the 1961 season, he held all the Giants' passing records.

In his first three seasons, 1970–72, this 49ers defensive end registered an amazing 10 sacks in five playoff games. One of the best pass rushers of his era, this two-time all-pro moved across the bay to Oakland in 1980 and played on a Super Bowl winner. Who is he?

This wide receiver from Rice was a real standout with the Steelers in the early 1960s. In his first five seasons he caught passes for 42 touchdowns and more than 4,700 yards, averaging 21.6 yards per catch. Injuries dragged him down after a trade to Dallas in 1964, however, and he caught only two TD passes in his last three seasons.

The leading rusher on the Lions' back-to-back championship teams in 1952 and '53 was a fine halfback who had started his career in 1946 as a tailback with the AAFC's Chicago Hornets. In a 10-year career he rushed for more than 4,500 yards and was a two-time all-pro selection. One interesting statistical note: After passing for 4,109 yards in four seasons in the AAFC, he threw only 26 passes in six years with the Lions and completed 11—10 of them for touchdowns. Who was the man they called "Hunchy"?

This great defensive end broke in with the Rams in 1971, Deacon Jones's last year in L.A., and picked up right where Jones left off. The mainstay of the Rams' defense throughout the '70s, he was an all-pro each year from 1974 through 1980. He missed one game in his career—in 1984, his final season.

 In a 17-year career this Stanford alumnus led the NFL once in passing, three times in passing yardage, and twice in TD passes. He never appeared in a Super Bowl, but he took the 49ers to the first two NFC championship games, where they lost to Dallas each time. Altogether he passed for 31,548 yards and 214 touchdowns. Do you remember him?

 This great tackle from Michigan was a first-team all-pro every year from 1944 through 1949. Other than Steve Van Buren, he may have been the key to the Eagles' dynasty in the late '40s. But the Hall of Fame selectors still haven't realized it.

Game 11

3rd Quarter

North of the Border

1. After four undistinguished seasons with the Lions, the Cardinals, and the Dallas Texans, this quarterback from Notre Dame went north to Saskatchewan in 1953 and led Western Canada in passing yardage in four of the next six seasons. His Canadian success earned him a return to the United States in 1960 with the Denver Broncos, and he didn't disappoint, leading the new AFL in passing yardage in 1960 and '62 before age caught up with him. Hint: His son, a fellow Notre Dame alumnus, was a star in the NBA in the 1980s.

2. This two-time MVP from the CFL joined the Rams as a 34-year-old "rookie" QB in 1985. The Rams went 11–5 and dethroned the 49ers in the NFC West, and made it as far as the NFC championship game before the Bears bounced them. The CFL import

had a pretty good regular season but completed only 16 of 53 passes for 116 yards in the playoffs, and a back injury the following season ended his career.

 A few years earlier, the Rams had lost a starting QB when he jumped to the CFL after throwing 30 TD passes for them in 1980. Returning in 1982 after a disappointing season with Montreal, he was never the same. He's probably best remembered as the Rams' starting QB in Super Bowl XIV against the Steelers.

 This halfback from Oregon State played with the Cardinals from 1955 through 1957 and doubled as a punter, averaging 40.4 yards per kick. Jumping to Canada with the Toronto Argonauts in 1958, he led the Eastern Division in punting six times over the next dozen years. Can you name him?

 The New York Yanks' starting quarterback for most of 1951, this ex-California Golden Bear played less a year later after the franchise moved to Dallas. When the team went belly-up, our man made his way north to the ORFU, Canada's third "major" league (or top minor league, depending on how you look at it). Leading the Kitchener/Waterloo Flying Dutchmen to three straight ORFU titles, he was the all-league quarterback each year from 1954 through 1957 and the MVP in 1954.

 This end from Ohio State caught an NFL-high 12 touchdown passes in 1950 with the Cardinals, including 5 in one game. Joining the Calgary Stampeders in 1951, he was the West's leading scorer two years in a row, starring as a receiver and kicker.

 Drafted in the fourth round by the Dolphins in 1971, this Notre Dame QB signed with the Toronto Argonauts instead. After three years as a CFL standout he signed with the NFL in 1974, though not with the Dolphins. Less than a decade later, he was the quarterback of a Super Bowl champion and the NFL's MVP.

This halfback from the College of the Pacific was a multipurpose reserve with the Bears in 1952 and '53. He did his best work as a kickoff returner, averaging 30.5 yards on 22 returns, one of them for a touchdown. Jumping to the Calgary Stampeders in 1954, he made the Western all-star team in his first season up north. Four years later, by now playing mainly as a defensive back for the Hamilton Tiger-Cats, he made the Eastern all-star team. He came back to the States to play in the AFL's inaugural season for the Raiders and made his final season a memorable one by intercepting nine passes and making the first all-AFL team. Who is he?

After a fine debut with the Cleveland Rams in 1942, this passer from Oklahoma spent the next three years in the service. After the war, he spent two years as the Packers' signal caller but lost the job following a dismal 1948 season. In 1950 he went north and found new life with the Winnipeg Blue Bombers. He threw for 67 touchdowns in a two-year period (1951–52) and led the Bombers to the Grey Cup game in 1950 and '53 but came up on the short end each time.

Cut by the Redskins in 1953, this rookie running back from North Carolina State went to Canada and led the East in rushing and scoring a year later. He joined the Giants in 1955, and when he retired after the 1964 season, he held the team's career rushing record. Later he coached the Giants, but with little success.

One of the key players in Canadian football history, this quarterback began his pro career in 1947 with the Hawaiian Warriors of the Pacific Coast League. After the season, he was one of 15 Warriors who were kicked out of the league for gambling. Unable to land a football job in the States, he hooked on with the Calgary Stampeders, the first Canadian team to make a serious effort to sign experienced American pros. Led by their new QB, the Stampeders went undefeated and won the Grey Cup, and soon every team in Canada was looking for talent south of the border. Though he never duplicated the success of that first year in Calgary, our man hung around through 1953. Who is he?

At the height of the Canadian raids on the NFL, the 1954 Redskins lost two of their mainstays to Calgary. One, Washington's starting quarterback a year earlier, was a bit of a disappointment up north, throwing for only eight touchdowns against 24 interceptions; the other, an outstanding defensive end, made the Western all-star team. Welcomed back by the NFL in 1955, they helped the Redskins improve to an 8–4 record and a second-place finish. Who were these two jumpers?

This versatile 5'5" running back broke in with the Winnipeg Blue Bombers in 1971, gaining 2,347 yards as a runner, receiver, and kickoff returner. He was even better a year later, amassing 2,530 combined yards and leading the league in rushing. Signed by the Patriots, he led the NFL in kickoff return yardage in 1973, then set a record (since broken) with 2,444 combined yards a year later: 824 rushing, 474 receiving, 517 in punt returns, and 629 in kickoff returns. But he was released in the middle of the following season; picked up by the Falcons, he finished out 1975 with them and never played in the NFL again.

In 1967 and '68 he passed for a total of 8,812 yards and 71 touchdowns with the Calgary Stampeders, winning the Canadian MVP Award in the latter season. That got the attention of several teams in the United States and earned him extended shots with the Broncos (1969–70) and the Eagles (1971–72). Having failed to set the NFL on fire, he went back to the CFL for three more years and called it quits after the 1975 season. Who is this Penn State alumnus?

This sophomore end with the Eagles ranked second among the NFL's receivers in 1952 with 56 catches for 997 yards. A year later he jumped to Winnipeg, where he led Western

Canada in receptions three times and later coached four Grey Cup champions before returning to the States for a long career as an NFL coach. Ironically, considering his Canadian triumphs, he's remembered here as a coach who couldn't win the big one.

Game 11

4th Quarter

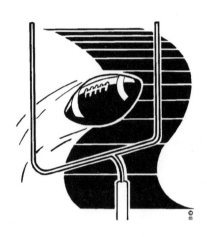

Nicknames

 1. L.T.

 2. The Mad Stork

3. Mean Joe

4. Mercury

5. The Minister of Defense

6. Night Train

7. Ox

8. Papa Bear

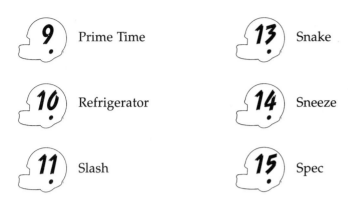

9   Prime Time

10   Refrigerator

11   Slash

12   Slingin' Sam

13   Snake

14   Sneeze

15   Spec

Game 12

1st Quarter

Moments to Remember

 In the 1963 AFL title game, this Chargers fullback rushed for 206 yards on just 13 carries, including gains of 56 and 67 yards; caught seven passes for 123 yards and a touchdown; and even completed a pass of his own for a 20-yard gain. It adds up to 349 yards of total offense, and nobody has ever done better in a championship game.

 A second-year running back from UCLA ran wild as the Jets routed Cincinnati 44–17 in the first round of the extended 1982 playoffs, gaining 211 yards on 22 carries and breaking the last man's playoff rushing record. After the game, though, it turned out that a 9-yard gain by Bruce Harper had been mistakenly credited to our man, and his revised total of 202 yards left him just short of the record. With the added clue that he was the NFL's leading rusher in that strike-shortened season, do you remember him?

Even if the Jets star's record had been allowed to stand, he wouldn't have held it for long, because three years later this star rushed for 248 yards on 34 carries, including touchdown runs of 55 and 40 yards, to shatter the playoff record as his team posted a 20–0 win over the Cowboys. If I tell you he was coming off the only regular season of his first four in which he didn't lead the NFL in rushing, can you tell me his name?

With just 28 seconds left in the 1950 championship game, his 16-yard field goal sailed through the uprights to give the Browns a 30–28 victory over the Rams.

In a Monday-night game early in the 1973 season, a Washington defensive back tackled a Dallas running back just short of the goal line on the final play to preserve a 14–7 victory. Can you name the Redskins defender, who's now in the Hall of Fame? And for extra credit, do you remember the Dallas back who couldn't quite escape his grasp?

The highest-scoring playoff game in NFL history was a 58–37 shootout in a first-round NFC matchup on December 30, 1995. If I tell you that Charlie Garner scored the first touchdown for the winners and that Don Majkowski came off the bench to throw three TD passes in a losing cause, can you tell me the two teams involved?

The first 300-yard passing game in the NFL was recorded in the final week of the 1937 season. A week later, playing on an ice-covered field in 15-degree weather, a rookie superstar shattered that record, passing for 354 yards and three touchdowns to lead his team to a 28–21 victory in the championship game.

All things considered, it may have been the greatest postseason passing performance ever. Can you name the future Hall of Famer who overcame the elements?

 With 12 seconds left in the first half of Super Bowl XVIII, the Redskins had the ball deep in their own territory, trailing the Raiders 14–3 and hoping to regroup at halftime. Rather than simply running out the clock, they tried a flat pass that was intercepted by a Raiders linebacker and returned for a touchdown that gave his team a lead that proved to be insurmountable. Who is this unheralded Raider, who in a five-year career intercepted only one other pass?

 The shortest overtime game in history occurred on Thanksgiving Day, 1980, in Detroit. The Lions' kickoff to start the extra period was returned 95 yards for a game-winning touchdown. What team beat the Lions that day? And for extra credit, who was the kick returner who showed the Lions the real meaning of "sudden death"? Hint: In a five-year career he returned three kickoffs for TDs.

 Who caught Joe Montana's pass in the end zone with just 34 seconds left in Super Bowl XXIII to give the 49ers a thrilling 20–16 victory over the Bengals?

 The Colts captured their first (and so far only) Super Bowl title by a score of 16–13 when this man nailed a 32-yard field goal with five seconds left in Super Bowl V.

 Earlier in that same game, the Colts scored their first touchdown when Johnny Unitas's pass bounced off the intended receiver, Eddie Hinton, then was tipped by a Dallas defensive back right into the hands of the Colts' tight end, who chugged into the end zone to complete a 75-yard play. Can you name the unlucky defensive back and the tight end who took advantage of the friendly bounce? Hint: Both are in the Hall of Fame.

Two years later, a similar play gave the Steelers the first playoff win in their history. Trailing the Raiders 7–6 with 20 seconds to go, Terry Bradshaw had a fourth-down pass broken up, but Franco Harris made a shoestring catch of the deflected ball and raced into the end zone for a 60-yard touchdown play that was soon known to all as the "Immaculate Reception." The Raiders protested loud and long that the ball had bounced off the intended receiver, not their defensive back, which would have made Harris's catch illegal according to the rules at the time. Can you name the Steelers back who was Bradshaw's original target, and the Raiders defensive star who may or may not have tipped the ball?

What linebacker from LSU picked off three passes as the Dolphins shut out the Jets 14–0 in the 1982 AFC championship game? One of his interceptions set up Miami's first touchdown, and he returned his last one 35 yards for the Dolphins' other score. He made exactly three regular-season interceptions in his eight-year career, all of which he spent with Miami.

The highest-scoring game in NFL history was played on November 27, 1966. Leading 69–41, the home team called time-out with just seconds remaining and kicked a field goal to make the final score 72–41. It was just the latest episode in a rivalry that was already three decades old at that time. What were the two teams involved?

Trailing the Browns by a touchdown and at his 2-yard line late in the fourth quarter of the 1986 AFC championship game, this quarterback led his team on a 98-yard drive to tie the game, then drove them to a winning field goal in overtime. The QB's reputation for late-game comebacks began with this game. Who is he?

Bart Starr's game-winning quarterback sneak with seconds remaining in the 1967 NFL championship game (also known as the Ice Bowl) was made possible by two Packers linemen who drove a Dallas defensive tackle off the line of scrimmage. Can you name the center and guard who made the play work? And who was the unlucky Cowboy they victimized?

Game 12

2nd Quarter

All in the Family

 One of college football's greatest players was a Heisman Trophy winner from Michigan who played with the Rams in 1946 and '47. In the 1970s his son was a star quarterback at UCLA. The son never played in the NFL but went on to a career as an actor in movies and television. Can you name this famous father-and-son team?

 The older of these two brothers, Walt was an outstanding linebacker who played in five championship games, all with the Browns, and five Pro Bowls. Years later, as head coach of the Jets, he fell one game short of a trip to Super Bowl XVII. His kid brother Lou, a defensive tackle, was on the losing side in the 1964 NFL title game and Super Bowl III. He played in two Pro Bowls in his own right and doubled as a left-footed kicker, scoring 955 points in his career.

 One or the other of these two brothers led the Bears (or Staleys) in scoring in each of their first six years of existence. The elder doubled as co-owner of the team until the early 1930s; his little brother led the NFL in scoring in 1924 and was second in the AFL of 1926. Who were these stars of the early years?

 In 1975 a Cardinals halfback rushed for 816 yards, caught 43 passes, and returned one punt and one kickoff for touchdowns. Eighteen years later his son, playing for the Browns, rushed for 611 yards, caught 63 passes, and returned two punts for touchdowns. Two years after that, switched to wide receiver by the Falcons, the son caught 104 passes.

 One of these siblings was the star running back on the Eagles team that lost to the Raiders in Super Bowl XV. Three years later his brother Cleo was a kick returner with the Raiders team that beat the Redskins in Super Bowl XVIII. A third brother, Tyrone, spent two years as a reserve running back with the Raiders in the '90s. What's their family name? And what's the first name of the Eagles star who was the best known of the three?

 Two of the best-known brothers of recent years were these siblings from Clemson, both of whom played in the defensive line. The younger earned all-pro mention six years in a row from 1989 to '94 with the Browns, but his older brother is probably more famous, having made a name for himself with his highly publicized exploits as the game's largest fullback in 1985. Who are they?

 These two defensive stalwarts played college ball at Notre Dame and went on to have fine careers in the NFL. Bob played from 1979 to '92 with the Patriots, Browns, and Raiders and got into a couple of Pro Bowls; Mike played from 1986 to '93 with Houston, Philadelphia, and Miami with slightly less success. All you need is their last name.

 In 1994 a Hall of Fame coach took his team to Cincinnati, where it opposed a team coached by his son. It was the first time a father and son had faced each other as head coaches on opposing sidelines. You shouldn't need the Hall of Famer's team to get this one.

 These two ex–Miami Hurricanes made their debuts in 1988. One, a wide receiver, has caught more than 500 passes for the Seahawks; the other, a defensive back, played with the Lions until joining his brother in Seattle in 1997. Their first names are fairly similar, and many people probably don't realize they're two different players. Who are we talking about?

 A tale of two linebackers: Sam finished a six-year career, all with the Patriots, in 1979; Byron played eight years, all with the Giants, beginning in 1981. What's their last name?

 These two brothers are distinguished by the fact that they spell their last name differently. The elder, Nelson, was a defensive back with Baltimore in the 1970s; his younger brother, Chuck, was a star running back with the Saints and the Chargers. What's their last name, in either spelling?

 Three brothers born in Mexico—Joaquin, Luis, and Max—had short trials as kickers in the NFL in the 1980s, but none of them ever played a whole season with the same team. However, they had a cousin who scored 874 points in an 11-year career, more than twice as much as the three brothers' combined total. His finest years came with the Oilers from 1985 through 1989. Can you supply the family name, plus the cousin's first name?

This trio of brothers didn't set the NFL on fire, but they all played in the Super Bowl. Archie and Ray, both from Ohio State, each played seven years, all with Cincinnati—Archie as a running back, Ray as a defensive back. They both took part in the Bengals' 26–21 loss to the 49ers in Super Bowl XVI. Keith spent five years with the Redskins, including a cameo role in the rout of Denver in Super Bowl XXII. What's the name of this football family?

One of the Chiefs' two first-round draft choices in 1963 was a guard who became a mainstay of their offensive line. Four times an all-pro, he started for them in two Super Bowls and played until 1976. His son, also a guard, was the Chiefs' top pick in 1980 and spent seven years in Kansas City before calling it quits after the 1986 season. Can you name them?

Game 12

3rd Quarter

Shooting Stars

 This quarterback really blossomed in his fourth season as a starter and was a unanimous all-NFC choice as he led the Redskins to the Super Bowl, where he won the game's MVP Award. By 1994 he had left Washington, and since then he's been a backup with a different team each year.

 This halfback from Syracuse had been bouncing around in pro football circles for three uneventful years when he got his first real shot in 1943 with the combined Phil-Pitt team and surprised everyone by gaining 571 yards on the ground, missing the rushing title by a single yard. He followed that with another good season in 1944, but for the rest of his seven-year career he was mainly a backup, and when he hung up his cleats, that 1943 season still accounted for more than half of his career rushing total.

A former Heisman Trophy winner who had been inconsistent for most of his NFL career, he blossomed in 1996, throwing for 4,177 yards and 33 touchdowns and earning his first trip to the Pro Bowl. A year later he lost his starting job in midseason to Eric Zeier.

In a six-year career with three different teams, he never gained as many as 500 yards rushing in any season, but in two championship games with the Browns, in 1952 and '53, he was a real standout. Moreover, he had the odd distinction of posting identical stats in each game: 15 carries, 104 yards, and one touchdown. The Browns lost both games, but it wasn't the fault of the man they called "Chick." What was his name?

Picked up by the Raiders in 1967 after a two-year hitch in the military, this wide receiver blossomed a year later, and from 1968 through 1970 he caught passes for 3,332 yards and 37 touchdowns, averaging 23 yards per catch. But he missed the 1971 season after being jailed for a parole violation and quit during training camp in 1972. Who is this true shooting star?

This backup quarterback completed only 31 passes in a three-year career, but two of them went for touchdowns on Thanksgiving Day, 1974. What's the big deal, you say? Well, he had replaced the injured Roger Staubach in a nationally televised game with the Redskins, and those two scores helped Dallas overcome a 13-point deficit for a thrilling 24–23 win. His resultant fame lasted only until the Cowboys' next game. He finished with the Chargers in 1976.

The Lions' first 1,000-yard rusher was a Heisman Trophy winner from Oklahoma who chalked up 1,035 yards in 1971 after an injury-plagued rookie season. He looked like a star for years to come, but the injury bug returned, and he gained less than 1,300 yards more before hanging up his cleats after the 1974 season. Do you remember him?

 The Packers thought they had found a franchise player when this third-year quarterback from Virginia passed for 4,318 yards and 27 touchdowns in 1989. But it was just a mirage; over the next seven seasons, including stops in Indianapolis and Detroit, he threw only 25 more TD passes.

 This third-year man from Arkansas had a breakthrough season in 1992 when he gained 1,690 yards for the Steelers, on a league-leading 390 carries. He was on a similar pace a year later when an ankle injury stopped him in midseason. Though he bounced back pretty well in 1994, his big contract made him expendable, and it turned out to be his final season.

 In his first two seasons with the Redskins, this fullback from Washington State rushed for a mere 179 yards. But in 1945 he exploded for 797, second only to Steve Van Buren, and made the all-pro team in helping the 'Skins to the Eastern Division title. He reverted to form in 1946, picking up 166 yards in his final season.

 Despite his back-to-back MVP seasons, Brett Favre still doesn't hold the Packers' single-season record for passing yardage. That belongs to the man who threw for 4,458 yards and 32 touchdowns in 1983, averaging an amazing 9.2 yards per throw. He also threw 29 interceptions, though, and that was his main problem during his six-year reign in the early 1980s as Green Bay's main man. With the added clue that he had lost an earlier battle with Dan Pastorini for the Oilers' starting job, can you name him?

This second-year Detroit end took off in 1950, hauling in 50 passes for 1,009 yards and 11 touchdowns, including a 302-yard, four-TD effort against Baltimore. He spent the next season in the service but returned in 1952 and picked up right where he left off, averaging 22 yards per catch and tallying 15 TDS. But he caught only 22 more passes before calling it quits after the 1954 season. Who was this two-year wonder?

 In 1985 and '86 this undersized back rushed for more than 2,800 yards and scored 35 touchdowns for the Giants, plus 313 more yards and four more scores in the playoffs after the 1986 season. But he tailed off badly after that, and a serious injury in 1989 kept him out of the game for two years. He tried a comeback with the Browns in 1991 but called it quits after the season. Who is this former Syracuse star?

 As the Bears' starter from 1990 through 1993, this quarterback from Michigan was best known as coach Mike Ditka's sideline whipping boy. But in 1995 he came out of nowhere to lead the NFL in passing and lead his new team to the AFC championship game, where they came within one play of a trip to the Super Bowl.

Game 12

4th Quarter

Men of Letters

 1. What quarterback who led his team to multiple Super Bowls told his story in *Armed & Dangerous*?

 2. *Fatso* is the story of this defensive tackle who had a Hall of Fame career with the Colts.

 3. What famous Packers playboy celebrated his off-the-field exploits in *Football and the Single Man*?

Known as intelligent and outspoken during his career with the Browns, this defensive back pulled no punches about the NFL in *They Call It a Game*.

 What former wide receiver put a fictional twist on his days with the Cowboys in a bestseller called *North Dallas Forty*?

 One Knee Equals Two Feet is just one of several books by this former coach who has proved equally successful as a broadcaster.

 In the Trenches is the story of one of the game's greatest defensive linemen.

 The inspiring account of this Hall of Fame running back's life is titled *I Am Third*.

 What great coach detailed his philosophy in *Run to Daylight*?

 What sportswriter learned the fine art of quarterbacking in *Paper Lion*?

 A standout defensive back with the Colts, Steelers, Redskins, and Jets, he told all in *Confessions of a Dirty Ballplayer*.

 What AAFC star who later became Otto Graham's backup with the Browns was the author of *Confessions of a Gypsy Quarterback*?

 For 1960s fans, the title of this one should give the author away: *I Can't Wait Until Tomorrow . . . 'Cause I Get Better-Looking Every Day.*

One of the game's greatest coaches recounted his career in *The Winning Edge.*

 Rise & Walk is the story of this Jets lineman's courageous recovery from a devastating injury.

 What two Miami running backs combined their literary talents in *Always on the Run*?

 What ex-Colts halfback displayed his talents as a raconteur in *My Story (And I'm Sticking to It)*?

 A Hall of Famer and later a broadcasting celebrity, this former Giant was the author of *The Whole Ten Yards.*

Game 13

1st Quarter

Coaching Carousel

 Perhaps the greatest testament to this Hall of Fame coach's ability is the fact that in a 12-year career he won three Super Bowls with three different quarterbacks. In another season he made it to the NFC championship game with a fourth QB.

 The Brooklyn Dodgers hired this famous Pitt coach in 1940, and he paid immediate dividends, finishing second two years in a row before joining the military in 1942, after which the Dodgers returned to their accustomed role as doormats. Back from the service, he took over the lowly Steelers in 1946, and in 1947 he led them to a first-place tie before losing a playoff to the Eagles—the franchise's only postseason appearance until the 1970s. But a brain tumor claimed the coach's life in the off-season, and the Steelers reverted to mediocrity.

What Hall of Fame coach was the first to call all of his team's plays from the sidelines? It was just one of his many innovations.

This man was the Coach of the Year with the Rams in 1973, the Bills in 1980, and the Seahawks in 1984. Though he never made it to the Super Bowl, he made a practice of taking over teams that were going nowhere and taking them to the playoffs with regularity.

The coach of the Portsmouth Spartans when they lost the famous indoor playoff game for the 1932 NFL title, he finally made it into the winner's circle three years later when his team, by now based in Detroit, beat the Giants for the championship. To that point he'd never had a losing record, but after a third-place finish with the Lions in 1936 he moved to Brooklyn and never finished on the plus side again in four more years as a head coach.

Fired just a few days after his team finished the 1968 season with a 10–3–1 record, this coach was rehired after a strong show of support from his players, only to be fired again two years later (after a 9–4–1 record). In 1978, after a successful stint with another team, he was rehired by his former club. This time, though, the players rebelled against his regime, and he was fired after just two preseason games. Who was this controversial coach?

Perhaps the least-remembered coach of a Super Bowl winner is this former Ohio State end who played a single season with the Giants in 1946. He took over the Colts after Don Shula's departure in 1970 and led Baltimore to an 11–2–1 record, followed by a victory in what may have been the sloppiest Super Bowl game ever. He guided the Colts to the AFC title game a year later but lost his job after a 1–4 start in 1972.

Another obscure Super Bowl coach is the man who made it there in his first season as the Broncos' head man, 1977, only to drop a 27–10 decision to the Cowboys. Fired after an 8–8 season in 1980, he gave the following reason for his dismissal: "Illness and fatigue. The fans were sick and tired of me." Still, his team made the playoffs in three of his four seasons. Can you name him?

 A famous story has it that in Sammy Baugh's first practice with the Redskins his coach described a pass pattern and concluded by saying, "And Sam, you hit him right in the eye with the ball." To which the young sharpshooter is supposed to have replied, "Which eye?" If indeed this ever happened, what Hall of Famer would have been the coach in question? Hint: In 11 years as a head coach—7 with the 'Skins and 4 in the AAFC—he reached the championship game six times, winning twice.

 What Hall of Fame coach is the only man to win championships in the NFL and the AFL, turning the trick with the Colts and the Jets?

 One of the AFL's original coaches, he won the last Super Bowl before the merger in 1970. His team compiled a regular-season record of 43–12–1 in the AFL's last four years of existence, but he had only one playoff team after the merger and was ousted after the 1974 season. Two seasons with the Saints did nothing to revive his reputation; still, three AFL titles plus that Super Bowl victory are nothing to sneeze at. Do you remember the creator of "the offense of the '70s"?

 As the coach of the expansion Tampa Bay Buccaneers, he had records of 0–14 and 2–12 in his first two seasons but won a division title in his fourth. He's mainly remembered, though, for his sense of humor, which he might have developed out of necessity in those early years. Possibly his most-repeated one-liner came when, after yet another loss, he was asked what he thought of his team's execution, and he responded, "I'm in favor of it."

 This Brooklyn-born coach won division titles in his first three years as the Giants' head man but lost in the championship game each time. In five more years with the Giants, he compiled a record of 24–43–3 and became perhaps the most unpopular sports figure in New York, at least in the fall.

 OK, it's time for a tough one. After three years at the helm with the Los Angeles Bulldogs, this coach took over as head man of the Detroit Lions in 1939 and finished with a 6–5 record. In the off-season, told by the owner to take Bulldog Turner in the first round of the draft, he chose Doyle Nave of USC instead and was promptly fired. Who was this former Tulsa coach who was nicknamed "Gloomy Gus"?

Game 13

2nd Quarter

AFL Pioneers

Joining the Bills in 1961, this guard was a mainstay of the Buffalo team that made three straight trips to the championship game in the mid-1960s. An all-AFL selection five times in a nine-year career, he played his college ball at Georgia Tech.

Just from a glance at his stats—198 receptions in a nine-year career from 1962 through 1970—you wouldn't imagine that this tight end was a star for the Chiefs. But blocking was his forte, and he did it well enough to earn five all-AFL selections. Do you remember this Michigan State alumnus?

After three seasons in the NFL, this 6'8" defensive end found a home with the Raiders in 1964. He played in three AFL all-star games in a career that lasted through 1971, but he was known mainly as one of the roughest characters in the league. Fans of the 1960s might recall that he knocked Joe Namath's helmet off with one often-replayed hit. Who was this enforcer with the handlebar mustache?

The AFL's punting leader in its inaugural season, he's one of a handful who played in each of the league's 10 seasons. Also a fine linebacker, he appeared in six AFL championship games— three apiece with the Chargers and the Bills.

Serving as a backup for George Blanda, this Cincinnati alumnus completed 133 of 254 passes for 2,480 yards and 21 touchdowns as the Oilers won the Eastern Division title in each of the AFL's first three seasons. The Broncos were so impressed that in 1964 they traded all-AFL defensive tackle Bud McFadin plus a draft choice just to "lease" the young quarterback for two years. Given a full-time shot he wasn't terrible, but he wasn't what Denver was hoping for, and in 1966 he was returned to Houston and never played regularly again. He was last seen with the Chiefs in 1969.

This defensive tackle broke in with the Patriots in 1961 and stayed with them for 11 years, including five all-AFL seasons. Standing only 6' tall and weighing 270 pounds, he might have been made into a nose tackle in a 3–4 defense if he'd come along a decade later. Who is the Southern Illinois alumnus with the "big city" name?

Starting with the Dallas Texans in the AFL's first season, this cornerback moved to Kansas City with the team in 1963 and moved to Oakland solo in 1965. Neither move hurt his effectiveness, nor did a shift to safety in the late '60s. A six-time all-AFL selection, he picked off 48 passes in a 10-year career, and in his first four seasons he was a fine kickoff returner, too. His son and namesake later played four years as a linebacker with the Browns.

This running back never matched the 948 yards he gained on the ground in 1964, when he was the AFL's Rookie of the Year. But he was a mainstay of the Jets' ground game until a torn Achilles tendon ended his career early in the 1970 season. His finest hour came in Super Bowl III, when he carried 30 times for 121 yards and the Jets' only touchdown. Who is this star from Ohio State?

The consensus all-AFL center in each year of the league's existence, he was also an all-pro selection in the first three seasons after the merger. Need more? Well, his number was 00 and he never missed a game in his 15-year career.

Who is the outstanding big-play receiver who caught 294 passes for Buffalo from 1960 through 1967? His best season was 1964, when he averaged an amazing 27 yards per catch as the Bills won their first championship; an injury a year later kept him on the sidelines as they won their second straight title game.

The Chargers' No. 1 pick in the 1961 draft, this defensive end was everybody's choice as Rookie of the Year and a consensus all-AFL selection. Hampered by injuries in his sophomore year, he bounced back with three more all-AFL seasons in a row but was shipped to the expansion Dolphins during the 1966 season and called it quits after that, though he was only 27. Who is he?

This defensive tackle from Grambling was taken by San Diego in the 15th round of that same 1961 draft and teamed with the last man to give the Chargers a pair of rookies on the all-AFL team. Just about the biggest player of his time, at 6'9" tall and 290 pounds, he repeated as an all-AFL choice in 1964 and '65 before being traded to Houston in 1966 after a salary dispute, and finished with the Chiefs in 1968. Who is this huge man who was nicknamed the "Big Cat"?

What second-year fullback from Mississippi State led the Oilers to the Eastern Division title in 1967, rushing for 1,194 yards? He followed that up with two more outstanding seasons but was injured in 1970 and gained fewer than 500 yards altogether in three seasons after the merger.

This versatile athlete started his pro career as a running back with the Dallas Texans in 1960. He was pretty good, too, especially as a receiver; in two seasons he caught 76 passes and averaged almost 16 yards per catch. But in 1962 he shifted to safety, and after a couple of years of adjustment he was an all-AFL or all-pro choice seven years in a row, a streak that ended in 1971, his final season. In 10 years as a defensive back, all with the Texans/Chiefs, he intercepted 57 passes. Who is this former LSU star?

Game 13

3rd Quarter

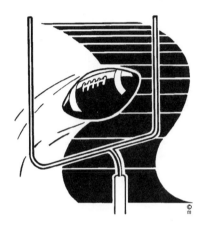

Draft Day

 1. Despite the exhaustive preparation that goes into the modern NFL draft, outstanding players still manage to fall through the cracks. One prime example is a defensive back from Grambling who joined the Cowboys in 1981 as an undrafted free agent and proceeded to lead the NFC in interceptions three times in the next five years. A four-time Pro Bowl selection, he picked off 57 passes in a 13-year career and was last seen with the Browns in 1993.

 2. Another standout who was overlooked on draft day in 1981 was this huge offensive tackle who signed with the Redskins and became perhaps the best of the Hogs. He played in four Pro Bowls and four Super Bowls in a career that lasted through 1993.

There were 442 players chosen in the 1970 draft, but this offensive lineman from South Dakota State wasn't one of them. Invited to camp by the Dolphins, he managed to win a job as a reserve guard, and in 1972 he moved over to become the starting center, where he was an all-pro each year from 1973 through 1977. Who is this Hall of Famer?

The Jets took Joe Namath with their first choice in the 1965 draft and signed him to a record-breaking $400,000 contract; in the second round they took another quarterback, a Heisman Trophy winner from Notre Dame, who signed a very lucrative $200,000 deal himself. Apparently the No. 2 pick was insurance, in case Namath's already damaged knees couldn't hold up under the strain of an NFL season. But Namath's knees did hold up, at least for a few years, and the Notre Dame man never played for the Jets. In the end he threw only 48 passes in a six-year career with four different teams. He was last seen with Memphis in the WFL, where he did have one good season as a starter in 1974. Can you name him?

The Packers spent about $1 million to sign a pair of first-round picks in 1966, hoping that these two All-American running backs could become the next Taylor and Hornung. One of them, from Texas Tech, turned out to be a fine player, exceeding 750 yards rushing three times for Green Bay and giving the Cardinals a couple of fine seasons; the other, from Illinois, had only two good years, in 1967 and '68, and was last seen with the Bears in 1971. And neither of them could do anything to stop the Packers' decline in the post-Lombardi years. Can you name them?

The Seahawks used a supplemental pick in the 1987 draft, giving up their No. 1 pick in 1988, to take this highly publicized linebacker from Oklahoma. But his high profile off the field wasn't matched by his performance on the field, and a shoulder injury finished him after the 1989 season. Who is this first-round flop?

John Elway, as you may recall, was not drafted by the Broncos, but by another team—a team he said he'd never play for. A few days after the draft, Denver acquired him for backup quarterback Mark Herrmann, a No. 1 pick in 1984, a million dollars, and the player the Broncos had just drafted with their own top pick, No. 4 overall. This is a two-part question, then: What team drafted Elway, and what offensive tackle, a seven-time Pro Bowl selection from Northwestern, was the main player in the package the Broncos traded for him?

The 1983 draft become known as the Year of the Quarterback because six QBS were taken in the first round. You know Elway was one of them; the other five were chosen by the Bills, the Chiefs, the Dolphins, the Jets, and the Patriots, respectively. Can you name them?

In 1946 the Redskins used their No. 1 pick to select a back from UCLA. Unfortunately they failed to realize that he was a junior, and ineligible for the draft. A year later they drafted him again, apparently unaware that he had already declared he wouldn't play professionally. When the UCLA star lived up to his vow, it meant Washington had squandered two first-round picks on the same player, a record for draft-day futility. Who was the player the Redskins wanted so badly?

The first player taken in the 1977 draft, this running back had one great year in 1979 with Tampa Bay, gaining 1,263 yards and averaging 4.5 per carry, then rushing for 142 more yards as the Bucs won their first playoff game. For the rest of his six-year career, all but the last year spent in Tampa Bay, he gained a total of 1,800 yards with a 3.3-yard average. Who is this one-year wonder from USC?

The most consecutive years a team has gone without a first-round draft choice is 11. The second-longest streak is seven years—by the same team! And since the second streak started only five years after the first one ended, altogether this team had three first-round picks in 22 years. It made the playoffs 11 times in that span, though, including four trips to the Super Bowl. What's the team?

The Cowboys managed to draft two quarterbacks in 1989 who had finished third and fourth, respectively, in the 1988 Heisman Trophy voting—one with the first pick in the draft, the other through a supplemental draft choice, which meant giving up their No. 1 pick for the following year. They split playing time just about equally in 1989 as Dallas suffered through a 1–15 season. One of them, of course, was Troy Aikman. Who was the other?

The first player chosen in the 1965 NFL draft, this running back from Auburn rushed for 659 yards as a rookie with the Giants but averaged only 3.4 yards per carry. Still, it was his best season in a six-year career marred by nagging injuries. He wasn't a complete bust, but the Giants had certainly hoped for a lot more from him.

The Redskins drafted this quarterback in the 11th round in 1945, when his college class graduated. However, he was in the service at the time, and when the war ended, he went back to school. In 1948, when he was finally ready to turn pro, the Redskins grabbed an Alabama All-American with their top choice, hoping to groom him as Sammy Baugh's successor. Suddenly the man from Ole Miss didn't figure in their plans, so they sent him to the Giants, where he immediately won the starting job and held it for years. The Alabama QB never played a full season as a starter and was last seen with the Lions in 1956. The Giants' QB should be easy, so you shouldn't take full credit unless you also know the man the Redskins chose to keep.

Game 13

4th Quarter

Before and After

 Heralded college quarterbacks sometimes have a tough time breaking into the NFL. But what about the incumbent QBS who are shunted aside to make room for the new glamour boys? No one has suffered more in this regard than the man who was bounced from three different teams in favor of Joe Montana, John Elway, and Vinny Testaverde, respectively. (He was also benched in favor of Steve Young, though in that case it was Young who was eventually sent packing.) But he bounced back to lead a fourth team into the playoffs in 1990.

 Another who suffered a similar fate was this Auburn quarterback who spent two years as the Jets' starter before the arrival of Joe Namath, then took most of the snaps for the Dolphins in their first season but lost his job a year later when Miami drafted Bob Griese.

 While we're talking about the Dolphins, what LSU alumnus took the Miami quarterback job from Griese in 1980 and held it until Dan Marino arrived in 1983?

 The Steelers began building their Super Bowl dynasty in 1969 when they hired Chuck Noll as head coach. Likewise, the Redskins began a string of playoff appearances when they hired George Allen in 1971. Another thing these two coaches had in common: They both replaced the same man. Who is the former Giants lineman who led the Steelers from 1966 through 1968 and the 'Skins in 1970?

 Mark Moseley scored 81 points and booted 18 field goals in 1974, his first year with the Redskins, but that fell short of his predecessor's totals by 22 points and four field goals. With the added clue that the man Moseley replaced led the NFC in scoring in 1971, can you name him?

 What quarterback from Oregon, the first player selected in the 1955 draft, suffered a broken kneecap early in the 1956 season and gave Johnny Unitas his shot at the Colts' starting job? Needless to say, our man never got his job back, but he later saw significant action with the Giants, the Vikings, and the Broncos.

 Who replaced Walter Payton as the Bears' workhorse back in 1988? It was the first of three straight 1,000-yard seasons for this former Florida Gator, but he faded quickly after that and called it quits after the 1993 season. Still, he rushed for 6,166 yards and caught 302 passes in an eight-year career.

After seven years as a backup and sometimes-starter with the Chiefs, this SMU product finally took over as the full-time quarterback in 1976 after Len Dawson retired. By that time, though, he was already 30 years old, and he held the job for only three mediocre seasons, then spent his final season back on the Chiefs' bench again. Do you remember him?

 Though he was named Coach of the Year in 1979 with the Redskins, this man is not fondly remembered in Washington, mainly because he had the bad luck to follow George Allen and be replaced by Joe Gibbs.

 Bart Starr became the Packers' full-time quarterback in 1961. For the previous four years he shared the job with two different journeymen from Kentucky and Arkansas, respectively. One was later a star in the AFL with the Patriots; the other had been the Cardinals' starter for several years in the 1950s. Who are they?

 From 1967 to 1993 the Chiefs employed only two kickers. The first scored more than 100 points in each of his first five seasons, stuck around through 1979, and totaled 1,231 points in a Kansas City uniform. His successor arrived in 1980 and scored 1,466 points in 14 seasons with the Chiefs. Both played a few years with other teams after leaving Kansas City, and today they rank second and third, respectively, on the career scoring list. Who are they?

 Albie Reisz and Tom Colella divided the tailback chores for the Cleveland Rams in 1944, but a rookie from UCLA forced them both to the sidelines a year later—though Colella resurfaced as a solid defensive back with the Browns in the AAFC in the late '40s. Who was the star who replaced them?

 What Redskins cornerback held out for the entire 1983 season and was replaced by rookie Darrell Green? Our man never played in the NFL again, and Green soon made even the fans in

Washington forget him. He might be better remembered in Tampa Bay, where he had previously enjoyed three solid seasons with the Buccaneers.

 What Maryland alumnus was the Steelers' starting quarterback for the two years before Terry Bradshaw's arrival?

 This fourth-year quarterback from Youngstown State became the Steelers' starter when an injury finished Bradshaw in 1983. A year later our man jumped to the USFL, where he had two outstanding seasons with the Birmingham Stallions; when that league folded, he came back to the NFL as a backup with the Cardinals.

 In 1972 Jerry DePoyster averaged 36.9 yards per kick in his second season as the Raiders' punter, which turned out to be his last. He was replaced in 1973 by a rookie who exceeded that average by more than eight yards. Who was the strong-legged rookie?

 What USC signal caller took over the Oilers' quarterback job after George Blanda was sent to Oakland in 1967? Though he had a miserable season statistically, the Oilers won the Eastern Division before being slaughtered by Blanda's new team in the AFL championship game. Hint: The new QB's brother later became a very successful general manager with the Redskins and the Chargers.

 What rookie from Alabama took over from Bart Starr as the Packers' starting quarterback in 1971, his rookie season? He didn't quite fill Starr's shoes, throwing for seven touchdowns and 17 interceptions, but a year later, although our man didn't do a whole lot better, the Pack won the NFC Central title, and he looked as if he might settle in as a solid starter. It didn't happen, though, and he finished up with the Lions in 1979, after two years as a sometimes-starter in Atlanta.

Game 14

1st Quarter

Yesterday's Heroes

 This linebacker broke in beside Sam Huff with the 1965 Redskins. In a 14-year career he was picked nine times for the Pro Bowl and six times as a first-team all-pro, several more than Huff in each case. But today Huff is in the Hall of Fame while this former Tar Heel is a dim memory, except in Washington.

 Perhaps an even better linebacker was this Cowboys star who's still the only player from a losing team to be named MVP in a Super Bowl. Can you name this West Virginia alumnus who was an all-pro each year from 1966 through 1971?

Yet another overlooked linebacking great was a 49er who was an all-pro five times in an 11-year career, including 4 years in a row from 1970 through 1973. He was also selected for seven Pro Bowls, but you'll rarely hear his name today outside the Bay Area.

This former Miami Hurricane was the best running back the Vikings ever had. A four-time all-pro, he starred for them from 1973 through 1978. He led the NFL in receptions in 1975 and scored 51 touchdowns from 1974 through 1976. Though stifled in three Super Bowl appearances, he still rushed for 860 yards in playoff games. He played out the string with the Patriots in 1980, just a shadow of his former self. Who is this former Rookie of the Year and Player of the Year?

At the same time the last man was starring for Minnesota, another versatile runner and receiver was doing yeoman's work for the Colts. A two-time all-pro selection, he led the league in receptions twice, in 1974 and '77. The last of his outstanding seasons came with San Diego in 1978, and like the last man he burned out quickly. Who is this Penn State star, last seen in a brief appearance with the Rams in 1980?

After a year as a rookie nonentity, this running back from Colorado State gained more than 5,500 yards for the Rams from 1973 through 1977, and added another 687 yards in the playoffs. Another workhorse back who faded quickly, he was last seen with Buffalo in 1981.

After a lackluster NFL debut in 1930, the Portsmouth Spartans vaulted into contention a year later on the strength of several new acquisitions. Two of the best were a guard from Texas who became a six-time all-pro and a tackle from Oregon who was an all-pro four times. No one seems to remember them these days, least of all the Hall of Fame selectors. But they helped the Spartans, and then the Lions, remain one of the NFL's strongest teams throughout the '30s.

After a couple of years with the Cardinals, one with the Bills, and one spent on the sidelines with a knee injury, this wide receiver joined the Vikings in 1976. In Minnesota he was a three-time all-pro selection, catching a high of 80 passes in 1979. His name was Bobby Moore when he broke into the NFL, but he changed it after his rookie season. What's the name he's known by today?

From 1968 through 1970 a wide receiver from Michigan State caught 129 passes for the Vikings and earned two trips to the Pro Bowl, on both of which he was joined on the all-star team by a 49ers receiver who had the same name. The Viking never had another good season, but the 49er had several, leading the league's receivers at various times in yardage, touchdowns, and average yards per catch. A three-time all-pro, he caught 385 passes good for 60 touchdowns in an 10-year career. What is the name these two shared?

The second pick in the 1971 draft, following a stellar college career at Ole Miss, this quarterback retired after the 1984 season having never played for a winning team in the NFL. Plagued by the inevitable injuries that come to QBs of woebegone teams, he threw for 125 touchdowns against 173 interceptions—but don't let that fool you. When he was healthy, and the team wasn't too bad, he was one of the best. The NFC Player of the Year in 1978, he may have had his best season in 1980 when he passed for 3,716 yards while playing for a 1–15 team.

The Rams never regretted grabbing this guard in the first round of the 1966 draft. He earned all-pro honors in 9 of the next 13 seasons, including his finale in 1978. Who is this former Michigan Wolverine?

This fine receiver from Louisville caught at least 53 passes for the Oilers each year from 1986 through 1993. Last seen with the new Jacksonville Jaguars in 1995, he caught 571 passes for 8,215 yards in a 10-year career.

Breaking in with San Diego in 1966, this wide receiver really came into his own in 1968, when he and Lance Alworth combined to give the Chargers a pair of 1,000-yard receivers. It was the first of four years in a row in which our man averaged more than 20 yards per catch, including a league-leading 22.9-yard average in 1970, when he also caught 12 touchdown passes. Last seen with Houston in 1977, he caught 405 passes for 7,538 yards. Do you remember this four-time Pro Bowl selection who was nicknamed "The Ghost"?

In the early 1970s this Falcons defensive end was one of the NFL's finest. The defensive Rookie of the Year in 1968, he was a six-time all-pro in 11 years with Atlanta, then finished his career with three years in Philadelphia, including an appearance in Super Bowl XV.

Game 14

2nd Quarter

Gridiron Tragedy

1. This four-time all-pro succeeded in the NFL despite never having played in college. One of the biggest defensive linemen of his day, as reflected in his nickname, he died of a heroin overdose in May 1963.

2. Few players, if any, came to a more tragic end than this offensive tackle who was an all-pro selection for 10 consecutive years. He finished with the Redskins in 1974 after playing 13 seasons with the Chiefs. Six years later, driven to depression by debt and a series of bad business moves, he killed himself and his wife. Who was this ill-fated star whose death shocked the football world?

This rookie from LSU was averaging better than 47 yards per punt for the Cardinals when he died in a plane crash on October 24, 1947.

 A year later the Cardinals suffered another major loss when an all-pro tackle from Texas died of a heart attack in the locker room after the season opener. Who was he?

 As a rookie with the Dolphins in 1983, this running back from Oklahoma averaged 4.6 yards per carry and was the team's third-leading rusher. But he was killed in a traffic accident just before training camp the following summer.

 A rookie guard with the New York Titans in the AFL's inaugural season, he suffered a broken neck October 9, 1960, in a game with the Oilers and died later that day.

 This large tackle was a unanimous all-pro selection in 1943, his second year with the Giants. He joined the service in 1944 but was able to play the last few games on weekend passes, including the championship game, which the Giants lost to the Packers. Just a few weeks later he was killed in action in the Vosges Mountains of France. Who was this two-time All-American from Georgetown?

 As a rookie with the Chiefs in 1964, he led the AFL in yards per carry. He followed with another excellent season a year later but suffered a minor knee injury late in the season and died of complications while undergoing surgery.

 This wide receiver for the Lions suffered a fatal heart attack on the field late in a game with the Bears on October 24, 1971. Never a starter, he was in his fifth NFL season, having spent the first three with the Eagles.

Gearing up to defend their 1963 championship, the Bears were stunned when an auto accident during training camp the following summer claimed the lives of two veterans. One was a reserve offensive end; the other was a speedy halfback known for his elusive runs. In seven years with the Bears he had rushed for nearly 3,000 yards, and his career seemed far from finished until disaster struck. Give yourself full credit if you can name the back, and take a bow if you know the end.

 After catching 26 and 25 passes, respectively, for the Cardinals in 1976 and '77, this tight end missed the whole 1978 season with a torn Achilles tendon. Returning to action in 1979, he died of heart failure during practice early in training camp. Who was this ill-fated end from Colorado?

 The previous man wasn't the only Colorado alumnus to die that summer. A month before training camp began, one of the Giants' starting defensive tackles was killed in a traffic accident. Who was he?

 What rookie running back from Grambling suffered a fatal injury in a preseason game in 1963? He was playing with the Chiefs, who had selected him in the 14th round of the AFL draft.

 This Heisman Trophy winner from Ohio State came into his own in 1955, his second season, leading the Redskins in rushing and finishing second in the NFL in scoring. But in training camp the following season he suffered brain damage in an auto accident, and he never played again.

 Tragedy struck the Redskins' training camp again a year later when this defensive back was fatally shot in a barroom brawl. A five-year veteran, he broke in with the Cardinals in 1952.

Game 14

3rd Quarter

Breaking In

1. This Michigan State All-American made a big splash in his debut with the 1939 Lions, rushing for 301 yards, completing 56 percent of his passes, and averaging 43 yards a punt. But he was never seen again in the NFL.

2. Miscast as a fullback for his first three seasons, this BYU product played almost exclusively on special teams until the Raiders made him a starter at tight end in 1982. Over the next six seasons he caught 438 passes, setting a record for tight ends with 92 in 1983 and breaking his own mark three years later. Who is this four-time all-pro?

The first player chosen in the 1964 NFL draft, this wide receiver averaged almost 20 yards per catch as a rookie with the 49ers, then led the league with 80 receptions, 1,344 yards, and 12 touchdowns a year later. He looked like a potential Hall of Famer after catching another 66 passes in 1966, but injuries hampered him for the next two seasons, and he was shifted to tight end when he lost a step or two. Though he played well with the Saints through 1972 and caught 360 passes in a 10-year career, he never recaptured the spark that made him a unanimous all-pro in his sophomore season.

Joining the Giants in 1935, this end from West Virginia led the NFL in receiving as a rookie. Known as something of a flake, he wore out his welcome after catching only seven passes in 1936.

The Redskins surprised a lot of experts when they made this Princeton alumnus, one of the first soccer-style kickers, their No. 1 pick in the 1966 draft. He silenced the skeptics by scoring 105 points in his rookie year and setting club records in every kicking category. But after a leg injury early in 1967, he never regained his touch, scoring only 165 points in his last five seasons. He finished with the Patriots in 1972.

Another kicker who fizzled after an outstanding rookie year was this Michigan product who booted a league-leading 35 field goals for the Giants in 1983 and tallied 127 points. After a leg injury the following year, he kicked only 41 more three-pointers over the next four seasons. Last seen in Super Bowl XXII, where he kicked six extra points in the Redskins' 42–10 rout of the Broncos.

The Bills thought they had their quarterback of the '70s when this 1970 rookie completed 55 percent of his passes for 2,507 yards. He never approached that yardage figure again, though, and by 1973 he had been replaced by another rookie. Who was this Buffalo bust?

This unheralded eighth-round draft pick from Morgan State spent his first two years as a reserve running back with the Browns, though he did shine as a kick returner. Jim Brown's unexpected retirement gave him a shot in 1966, and he responded with three consecutive 1,000-yard seasons, leading the NFL twice in rushing yards and once in scoring. Though he tailed off a bit after that, he amassed 7,274 yards on the ground in a 10-year career with Cleveland that eventually earned him a spot in the Hall of Fame.

Another running back who waited for his chance was this Seattle Seahawk who spent two years as a kick returner before exploding for 1,017 yards rushing in 1992. It was his first of four straight 1,000-yard seasons, with a high of 1,545 in 1994.

A major part of the Chicago Cardinals' youth movement in 1934, this halfback from Kansas State led the league in rushing a year later, though he failed to score a touchdown. A succession of injuries reduced him to a part-time player after that, and though he hung on until 1939, he never approached the level of his first two years.

In 1956 this rookie halfback gained 756 yards rushing, sixth best in the NFL. He gained only 128 more in the next 11 years, but there's a good reason: he was moved to end in 1957 and finished his career with 305 receptions. He broke in with the Browns but also had good years with the Steelers and the Redskins.

Fresh off the TCU campus, this rangy end led the NFL with a record 58 receptions in 1940 with the Eagles. He set another record with 14 catches for 180 yards in the season finale against the Redskins. But without Davey O'Brien to throw to him, he caught only 17 more passes over the next two seasons before departing.

The Redskins thought they had a keeper when this rookie from Notre Dame rushed for 1,063 yards in 1993, averaging a fine 4.8 yards per carry. But he lost his starting job early in the next season and never played regularly again.

 The NFL Rookie of the Year in 1974 was a Chargers back who rushed for 1,162 yards and averaged a whopping 5.1 yards per carry. An injury cost him most of the following season, and though he bounced back with three decent years from 1976 through 1978, he never regained his rookie form. He finished up with the 49ers in 1980.

 This All-American from Michigan State may have been the AFL's best linebacker in his first three seasons with the Oilers, making everybody's all-pro team from 1967 through 1969. Injuries caught up with him after that, though, and he bounced to the Steelers and the Patriots before hanging it up after the 1976 season.

 As a rookie in 1939 with the Cleveland Rams, this tailback led the NFL in passing, rushed for 458 yards, finished among the punting leaders, and won the MVP Award. He played effectively with the Rams through 1942 but was injured playing football for a military team during World War II, and when he came back with the AAFC 49ers in 1946, he was just a shadow of his prewar self. Who is this star from Mississippi?

Game 14

4th Quarter

Teams

For years teams had used a no-huddle offense for the two-minute drill at the end of the game or the first half, but in 1988 one AFC team started using it as early as the opening kickoff. In an era of increasing situational substitutions, the hurry-up offense caused major headaches for defenses, and before the playoffs the NFL essentially outlawed it, though it was clearly within the rules. That didn't stop the no-huddle team from advancing to the Super Bowl. What team are we talking about, and who is the coach who devised the system?

The last team faded after its trip to the Super Bowl, but another AFC team picked up the no-huddle system (dubbing it the

"K-gun") and used it very successfully over a period of several years. As before, you need the team and its head coach too.

 What was the last team to win the NFL championship that's not a current member of the league?

 At the other end of the spectrum, what was the last NFL team that failed and had to return its franchise to the league?

 During a championship season in the 1980s, members of what team recorded a rap song called "The Super Bowl Shuffle"?

 The 1972 Miami Dolphins, of course, are the only NFL team to go undefeated through the regular season and the playoffs. Earlier, though, another team had a pair of undefeated seasons spoiled when it came up short in the championship game. If I tell you it happened in 1934 and 1942, can you tell me the team?

 What team of the 1970s, a loser in its only Super Bowl appearance, was known as the Over the Hill Gang? And who was the coach whose personnel moves gave rise to the nickname?

 Another Super Bowl loser of the '70s was led by a defense known as Orange Crush. Like the team in the last question, this one made several more trips to the Super Bowl in the 1980s and '90s.

 What dynasty of the 1950s had an outstanding defensive backfield known as "Chris's Crew"? Moreover, can you name the two Hall of Famers in this group?

 Due to the shortage of players during World War II, the Steelers and the Eagles combined in 1943 to form the Phil-Pitt "Steagles." Despite the odd name, the resulting amalgamation wasn't bad at all, finishing with a 5–4–1 record. The Eagles wanted to fly solo in 1944, though, and the jilted Steelers combined with another team on the rebound. But this partnership failed to win a single game. What was the second team that joined forces with Pittsburgh?

 In recent NFL history, what team had an army of hard-core fans that sat in the end zone and dubbed their section the Dawg Pound?

 What team had a devoted band that stayed together for more than a dozen years after the franchise deserted its home city? (The band is still together, in fact, but is changing its name in 1998 in honor of a new team in town.)

 This team wasn't the first in the NFL to have a fight song, but theirs was the first to be widely recognized, and today it's still the best known in pro football. If I tell you the song was written in 1938 with lyrics by the owner's wife, can you tell me the team?

 This team got off to a great start in its first year in a new city, winning its first 10 games—the first 7 of them by shutouts. The season unraveled after that, with 3 straight losses, each by only a field goal, and the team ended up in second place. But that outstanding beginning had established a solid following in its new home, and it's still there today, 64 years later. What team are we talking about?

Game 15

1st Quarter

Minor Leagues and Others

1. This running back from little Bluefield State played in the three top leagues of the '60s—UFL, CoFL, and ACFL—from 1963 to '71, then resurfaced in 1974 in the WFL with the Philadelphia Bell, gaining 927 yards on the ground and catching 46 passes. Combining his minor league seasons with his two in the WFL, he rushed for more than 7,000 yards and more than 50 touchdowns in 10 years, without ever playing in the NFL.

2. During the NFL's ban on blacks from 1934 through 1945, a number of black players still found employment in high-level minor leagues. The Pacific Coast Football League was the most receptive in this regard, and at least two dozen blacks played in the PCFL in the early '40s. The best of them was Kenny Washington, a UCLA All-American, but not far behind him was a triple-threat tailback from the University of San Francisco who starred for the Oakland Giants from 1943 through 1946 and was named the league's MVP in 1945, beating out Washington for the award. Before the 49ers arrived in 1946, he was the Bay Area's biggest pro football star.

 Another black star in the early years of the PCFL was a tailback who was a teammate of Kenny Washington at UCLA. He joined the Los Angeles Bulldogs for a couple of games late in 1941, then again in 1944 after getting out of the service. His pro football career lasted just a handful of games, but he soon went on to bigger and better things in another sport. Who was this trailblazer?

 Black players didn't have as many opportunities in the East, but this college star from Iowa had two fine seasons with the Paterson Panthers of the American Association. A good runner and a fine receiver out of the backfield, he was a second-team all-league choice in 1937; then, after sitting out the following season, he returned in 1939 and made the all-league first team. Can you name him?

 Cut by the Falcons in 1969 after playing only one game, this rookie linebacker caught on with the Alabama Hawks of the Continental League, where he was shifted to center. He learned the new position so well that he went on to play 17 more years with the Falcons, including five trips to the Pro Bowl. Who was this Kentucky alumnus?

 Another CoFL rookie in 1969 was an offensive lineman from Notre Dame who made his debut with the Chicago Owls and went on to play 14 years with the Dolphins. A six-time Pro Bowl selection, he was preceded in the CoFL by his brother, a linebacker who played with the Philadelphia Bulldogs in 1965

and later played five years in the NFL, plus one season in the WFL. Take full credit if you know the Dolphins star, and give yourself a bonus if you can name his brother.

7. The Wilmington Clippers of the American Association had a pair of all-league ends in the late 1930s and early '40s who also enjoyed considerable success in the NFL. One had led the NFL in receptions in 1935; the other, a sandlot player with no college experience, parlayed his years with the Clippers into a successful career with the Philadelphia Eagles, for whom he starred in their glory years in the late 1940s. Take full credit if you can name either one.

8. The Cleveland Rams of the 1936 AFL had a standout end from Ohio State who led the league in touchdown receptions. It was the only season he played as a professional, but he went on to a Hall of Fame career as a coach. He coached teams that reached the championship game five times in the NFL and AFL (though winning just once) and was known as one of the game's great offensive innovators.

9. Considered the "minor league Joe Namath" for his lifestyle, if not his ability, this quarterback from Maryland came as close to being famous as a minor league football player could. His major league career consisted of two games with the Patriots in 1968, but from 1966 through 1971 he played with five different teams in the Atlantic Coast League, usually leading in completions, yardage, and touchdowns. He reappeared in 1974 with the WFL's Philadelphia Bell and led the league with 31 TD passes. His parents named him Sean Patrick, but ACFL fans knew him as "King."

10. This end led the Atlantic Coast League in receptions, yards, and touchdowns two years in a row before joining the Giants in 1970. He led the NFC in receptions a year later, becoming the first tight end to do so, and caught more than 400 passes in the NFL before finishing with the Vikings in 1980.

The AFL of 1940–41 had its only moment in the sun on October 19, 1941, when two great college stars made their debuts with the New York Yankees in a game against the Columbus Bullies. One, a halfback from Michigan, was the most celebrated college player since Red Grange; the other was a two-time All-American as a Texas A&M fullback. They joined the service shortly thereafter, and though each played a few years after World War II, they never duplicated their college successes with the pros.

The Spokane Shockers of the Continental League had a left-handed rookie quarterback in 1968 who completed 17 of 41 passes for a paltry 125 yards, with three interceptions. There was little indication that he was destined to be selected as the NFL's Player of the Year in 1974 and again in 1976. Who is this Alabama alumnus?

Another CoFL team in 1968, the Michigan Arrows, employed a kicker who had been cut by the Lions after two undistinguished seasons. He scored 25 points for the Arrows and did double duty as a punter, averaging a mere 36.1 yards on 33 kicks. Given another shot in the NFL, he scored 442 points from 1970 through 1973 and played on two Super Bowl winners. Last seen with Tampa Bay in 1981, he finished his career with 1,074 points. Who is this little man from Cyprus?

In 1947 this former Eagles back had perhaps the best all-around season any minor league star ever had. Playing for the Bethlehem Bulldogs, who won the AFL championship, he led the league in rushing, averaging 7 yards per carry; he topped all scorers with 96 points (an AFL record); he caught 15 passes for 7 touchdowns and an average of almost 35 yards per catch; he finished among the leaders in punting and interceptions; and he completed 7 of 12 passes for 176 yards. Even if I tell you that his nickname was Buzz, you probably won't know him; but you have to admit he had one heck of a year.

This quarterback got his only NFL shot in 1966, when the injury-riddled Giants picked him up after he led the Continental League in passing. He compiled much better stats than his predecessors with the Giants and seemed to have won a permanent spot, but he broke his leg in training camp a year later, missed the whole season, and went back to the CoFL in 1968. A two-time passing leader, he starred from 1963 through 1969 in the three best minor leagues of the period, with one year off for the injury. Who was this man with the major league arm and minor league luck?

Game 15

2nd Quarter

Teammates

 The Cardinals had an outstanding pair of ends who helped them make two trips to the championship game in 1947 and '48. One, a former Texas Longhorn, led the NFL in receiving yardage both years and led with 14 touchdown receptions in 1948; the other, from SMU, had been a standout since before the war. Both of them enjoyed two all-pro seasons, and the Texas alumnus was chosen by *Pro Football Illustrated* as the league's MVP in 1947. Can you name this dynamic duo?

 Another stellar pair of ends made Otto Graham's life easier for the first seven years of the Browns' existence. One of them, a six-time all-pro, caught 349 passes in that period, including a league-leading 62 in 1952, after which he went to Canada. His partner, a four-time all-pro himself, lasted four more years with the Browns and finished with 386 receptions, which eventually earned him a spot in the Hall of Fame. Who were these pass catchers extraordinaire?

O. J. Simpson gained 2,003 yards in 1973 running behind a Buffalo offensive line that had its own nickname, though only the two guards achieved any real notoriety in their own right. Do you remember the moniker shared by the Bills' linemen? Give yourself extra credit if you can name the guards.

Who were the Redskins' starting offensive linemen in 1982, the year they became known as the Hogs?

Dan Marino's favorite targets in his early years with the Dolphins were a pair of diminutive receivers known as the Marks Brothers. Their two best seasons came in 1984, when they combined for 2,695 yards and 26 touchdowns, and 1986, when they combined for 2,463 yards and 21 TDs. Can you name them?

What three Broncos receivers were known as the Three Amigos? Hint: Two of them had long and successful careers, but the third, who joined the team in 1987, had his second and last good season in 1988.

The Broncos lost Super Bowl XXII to a Washington team whose wide receivers had a nickname of their own. What trio of Redskins made up The Posse?

The 1982 Dolphins' defense, which shut out the Jets in the AFC championship game and held them to a mere 139 yards, was known as the Killer Bees because six of its starters had last names that started with B. Give yourself full credit if you can name four of them. Hint: Two were brothers.

A decade earlier, the Dolphins' great teams of the early 1970s featured one of the best tandems ever at safety. One had joined the team in 1968 and was all-pro from 1972 through 1974; the other arrived in 1970 and was all-pro from 1971 through 1975, while also doing a fine job as a punt returner. Who are they?

The Cowboys also had a fine pair of safeties in the 1970s. One was a six-time all-pro who retired after the 1979 season at only 31 years of age; the other, a two-time all-pro, lasted through the 1981 season. Can you name them?

What trio of fullbacks made up the Rams' Bull Elephant backfield in 1951? The combination was broken up when one of them went to the ill-fated Dallas Texans in 1952, but the other two hung around with the Rams through 1955 and 1957, respectively.

Though they're generally remembered as chronic losers, the Saints actually had a very good team from 1987 through 1992, compiling an overall record of 62–33 in those years. Their greatest strength was a terrific corps of linebackers—four of them, since they used a 3–4 defense. Each of them enjoyed several all-pro seasons, two of them are among the career leaders in sacks, and one was chosen as defensive Player of the Year in 1991. Can you name them?

The Steelers' first two Super Bowl winners featured the best trio of linebackers any team has ever had. Altogether they were selected to the Pro Bowl 24 times, and two of them are in the Hall of Fame. Not too many clues here, but it shouldn't take much to help you remember these guys.

In his first year as head coach of the Eagles, Buddy Ryan tried the unique experiment of using his quarterbacks the way many coaches use running backs: one playing on first and second downs, another on third downs and long-yardage situations. It didn't work very well, but do you remember the two QBS?

Dallas coach Tom Landry tried something similar with the Cowboys in 1962, shuttling two quarterbacks in and out of the game on every play. Like the previous pair, one was a veteran and the other was young and inexperienced; unlike the Eagles' twosome, each member of this pair had a good season, as they combined for 31 touchdowns against 17 interceptions. Can you name the Dallas duo?

Game 15

3rd Quarter

Notorious

Throwing 30 interceptions in a season is a quarterback's nightmare. It's happened 11 times, but despite what you might think, the guys who did it weren't a bunch of bums. Three are in the Hall of Fame, including the only man to make the list twice. I'll list the team each QB played for, the season, and the number of passes he had picked off; see if you can fill in their names.

 1947 Bears, 31

 1961 New York Titans, 30

 1960 Broncos, 34

 1962 Oilers, 42

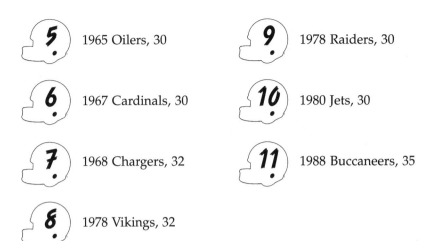

5 1965 Oilers, 30

6 1967 Cardinals, 30

7 1968 Chargers, 32

8 1978 Vikings, 32

9 1978 Raiders, 30

10 1980 Jets, 30

11 1988 Buccaneers, 35

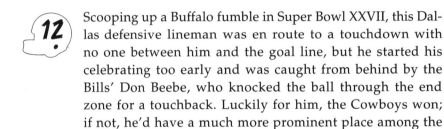

 12 Scooping up a Buffalo fumble in Super Bowl XXVII, this Dallas defensive lineman was en route to a touchdown with no one between him and the goal line, but he started his celebrating too early and was caught from behind by the Bills' Don Beebe, who knocked the ball through the end zone for a touchback. Luckily for him, the Cowboys won; if not, he'd have a much more prominent place among the game's goats.

 13 In three consecutive championship games in the 1960s, this Hall of Fame quarterback completed 35 of 90 passes for just 409 yards and one touchdown, with 10 interceptions. Not surprisingly, his team lost all three games.

14 Taking the field for its first possession in a Super Bowl game against the Redskins, the opposing team found it was without its all-pro running back, who had somehow misplaced his helmet on the sideline. The foul-up had no effect on the game, but over the years it came to symbolize the fortunes of this star-crossed team. Who was the unfortunate back who missed that first series, and what was the team he played for?

A defending Super Bowl champion of the 1980s lost its quarterback when a ridiculously flagrant late hit by a Packers lineman dislocated his shoulder. You shouldn't need the team to remember the often-injured QB whose absence killed its chances of repeating. Take extra credit if you know the lineman whose dirty play was the most notable moment in an otherwise undistinguished five-year career.

Game 15

4th Quarter

Milestones

Jim Brown's season record of 1,863 yards rushing stood for 10 years, until O. J. Simpson broke it in 1973. Simpson's mark of 2,003 yards lasted 11 years, until a second-year star from SMU racked up 2,105 yards in 1984. Though he's held the record longer than Brown or Simpson did, his reputation has faded rather quickly. Who are we talking about?

What Hall of Fame quarterback threw a record seven touchdown passes for the Bears in a 56–7 rout of the Giants in 1943?

Another Hall of Famer, this one playing for the Giants, matched that record in 1962 when he connected for seven TDs in a 49–34 win over the Redskins, throwing for 505 yards in the process.

He retired after the 1979 season with 81 career interceptions, a record that still stands. Even without that mark, you'd think seven years as a first-team all-pro and eight appearances in the Pro Bowl would have guaranteed him a spot in the Hall of Fame, but it took more than a decade until he was finally inducted in 1998. He played in four Super Bowls, but never on a winning team, and led in interceptions twice, once with the Redskins and once with the Vikings.

The single-season mark for interceptions is one of the most enduring in the NFL record book. It was set in 1952 by a rookie who picked off 14 passes and returned them for 298 yards and two touchdowns. He led the league again in 1954 and finished in 1965 with 68 for his career, still the third-best total of all time. Known as one of the hardest-hitting defensive backs who ever played the game, he broke in with the Rams but spent most of his career with the Cardinals and the Lions.

Known for the large amounts of "stickum" he smeared over his hands before each game, this Raiders defensive back put the sticky substance to good use in 1980. He picked off 13 passes and returned them 273 yards, both league-leading figures, then made five more interceptions in the playoffs, including one he returned for a touchdown. That makes 18 interceptions in a single season, and nobody's ever matched it.

The first to intercept as many as 40 passes, this USC alumnus picked off 41 in a short six-year career from 1949 through 1954. He had three seasons with 10 or more interceptions and retired as the career leader, though few took any notice at the time. He played his first four seasons with the Lions, then spent one year apiece with the Redskins and the Rams. He also played in four Pro Bowls.

The first back to rush for 5,000 yards in his career was this LSU alumnus who was the NFL's dominant player of the late 1940s.

The last man's rushing record was shattered by a 49ers star who amassed nearly 10,000 yards in a career that lasted from 1948 (in the AAFC) to 1963. He was also the first to have back-to-back 1,000-yard seasons.

The first passer to complete more than 60 percent of his passes, he connected 61.9 percent of the time in 1939. No, it's not Sammy Baugh, but he did play for the Redskins.

The first to complete 70 percent of his passes was Sammy Baugh, who did it in 1945. That record stood until 1982, when it was broken by a Bengals star who led the league in passing for the fourth time in his career. Who is he?

The first NFL passer to top 3,000 yards in a season did it in 1960, picking up 3,099 yards while leading the league in touchdown passes for the fourth year in a row. It was actually a disappointing season, since his team failed in its quest for a third straight championship. Who is this all-time great?

The first to break 4,000 was this AFL bomber who threw for 4,007 yards in 1967, only his third season.

To date, only one NFL passer has topped 5,000 yards in a season; it happened in 1984, a year when he also threw for 48 touchdowns, another record. All things considered, it was probably the best year any passer has ever had, and he had many other outstanding ones afterward, too.

Game 16

1st Quarter

All in the Family

 In 1946 and '47 the Bears' depth chart at fullback included these two brothers from Holy Cross. The better known of the two played his whole career with the Bears and was the NFL's rushing leader in 1939; his younger brother finished in 1949 with the New York Bulldogs. Who were they?

 In the early 1970s the Rams' defensive line featured this brother act. One was a great defensive tackle who played his whole 15-year career in L.A.; his younger brother lasted four years with the Rams and bowed out after two years with the Broncos.

These two brothers from Maryland weren't exactly stars in the NFL, but they played a combined 24 years at tight end in the 1980s and '90s. Kid brother John spent his whole career with the Saints; Mike played most of his 14 seasons with the Seahawks after making a successful switch from college quarterback to pro tight end. What's their last name?

After playing college ball at Texas, these twins joined the NFL in 1991 with the Steelers and the Colts, respectively, each playing tight end. One spent several years with the Chiefs; the other stuck with Indianapolis through 1994, then played with the Raiders and the Bears.

For a change of pace, how about a father-son combination? Junior was an all-AFL wide receiver who played for the Jets in their Super Bowl win over the Colts; three decades earlier, Senior was one of the leading rushers for the Packers team that won the NFL title in 1936. What's the name they shared?

Both members of this father-son team achieved some notoriety, though not for the same reason. Dad led the NFL in receptions as a rookie in 1940; his son, a running back with four different teams in the 1960s, is better known, but not for anything he did on the field. Instead, this free spirit is remembered as perhaps football's greatest flake.

These three brothers all enjoyed substantial careers in the NFL. Bill, the oldest, was a Penn State product who played linebacker for four teams from 1962 through 1970. His younger brothers, a pair of twins from Michigan State, each played a dozen years, from 1970 through 1981. Rich spent his whole career with the Rams and played in six Pro Bowls; Ron divided his career evenly between the Oilers and the Redskins. What's their last name?

These two Iowa alumni were among the league's better offensive linemen in the 1980s and early '90s. The elder, a center, played 11 of his 13 seasons with the Bears, and played in six Pro Bowl games. His brother, a center and guard, played 10 seasons, all with the Saints, and went to the Pro Bowl once. They both retired after the 1993 season, which they spent as teammates in New Orleans. Can you name them?

Two more solid offensive linemen of recent vintage were these brothers from Colorado. Pete spent his whole 12-year career with the Patriots, playing everywhere on the line; Stan, a tackle, played 13 years with the Saints and finished with the Chargers in 1995. A third brother, Willie, also from Colorado, played four games with the Lions in 1978. What's their family name?

Two brothers from William and Mary played together on the Cardinals' offensive line in 1950 and '51. The latter season was the last for the elder, a three-time all-pro; the younger was last seen with the Redskins in 1953. To confuse things, there was a defensive back on the 1950–51 Cardinals who had the same last name as these brothers but wasn't related. Give yourself full credit if you can name two of the three players we're talking about.

Here's one from the early years. Ernie Nevers's 1926–27 Duluth Eskimos featured three brothers who never played college football but played several years in the NFL. In fact, Duluth had employed at least two of these siblings each year since 1923. Their first names were Bill, Cobb, and Joe. Can you supply their last name?

The elder of these two brothers had a Hall of Fame career as a guard with the Raiders. His younger sibling spent nine years as a defensive lineman with the Browns, Chiefs, and Cardinals. If you need a hint, the Hall of Famer became a major figure in the players' association after hanging up his cleats.

Each of these brothers has had several all-pro seasons, and in 1993 they were both consensus choices, at wide receiver and tight end, respectively. If not for a bad break that sidelined the elder in midcareer, they might have lined up on opposing sides in Super Bowl XXXII. Who are they?

In 1951 the Browns had a versatile all-pro halfback who tied a record by scoring six touchdowns in a single game. Twenty-five years later, his son was an all-pro quarterback for the Colts, throwing for 3,104 yards and 24 touchdowns with only nine interceptions. Can you name this outstanding father-son team?

Game 16

2nd Quarter

Spring Fever

 1. A running back with the L.A. Express in 1984 and '85, this Purdue product blossomed in the NFL as a punt and kickoff returner, leading the league twice in each. An eight-time all-pro with the Saints and the Lions, he led the league in both categories in 1991. He's also the career record holder in kick-off return yardage, almost 3,000 yards ahead of the No. 2 man.

 2. The all-USFL center in 1985 with the New Jersey Generals, he was an all-pro each year from 1988 through 1991 with the Bills. A starter in four Super Bowls, he retired after the 1996 season.

The run-and-shoot offense got its start in 1984 with the Houston Gamblers. Can you name the head coach and the offensive coordinator who installed the system? And while we're at it, who was the Gamblers' rookie quarterback who passed for a record 5,219 yards and 44 touchdowns?

This quarterback started his career in 1969 with Indianapolis of the Continental League, won the MVP Award, and led his team to a 44–38 overtime victory in the championship game. Resurfacing in 1975 with San Antonio in the WFL, he led the league in passing yardage and TD passes. That earned him a shot in the NFL with the Eagles, but he threw only 65 passes before being cut loose after the 1979 season. Though he was 35 when the USFL started, he passed for more than 7,300 yards in 1983 and '84 with the Boston/New Orleans Breakers before calling it quits for the last time. Who is he?

A defensive end who broke in with the Philadelphia Stars in 1984 went on to become a star in the NFL, earning four trips to the Pro Bowl. In 1991 he had 15 sacks for the Oilers; in 1995 and '96, with the Eagles, he had 13 each year. He was still playing in 1997, but with a new team. Who is this former North Carolina Tar Heel?

The only thing that kept this running back from gaining 1,000 yards in each of his first four seasons was the 1982 strike. A two-time all-pro with the Bills, he jumped to the Birmingham Stallions in the spring of 1984 and led the USFL with 1,467 yards rushing. Returning to the NFL after the upstart league folded, he had a couple of decent seasons with the 49ers and was last seen with the Dolphins in 1988. Who is this former Auburn star?

The USFL's receiving leader in 1984 and '85, he caught 218 passes for 2,839 yards and 29 touchdowns over two seasons. Snubbed by the NFL except for a single game with the Redskins' "replacement" team in 1987, he finally got a shot with the Lions in

1989 and caught 70 passes for 1,091 yards. He snagged 64 a year later but vanished after that, probably forgotten by all but USFL mavens and Detroit fans. Do you remember this 5'7" star?

 Here's an easy one: What New Jersey Generals superstar set a pro football record when he rushed for 2,411 yards in 1985?

 The Packers dropped this offensive lineman after an unimpressive rookie year in 1980, but the Birmingham Stallions gave him a second chance in 1983. Shifted from tackle to guard, he became possibly the best lineman in the USFL for the next three years and was an easy choice for every all-league team. After the league folded, his only other NFL shot came in 1987 with the Steelers, who switched him back to tackle, then dumped him after the season. Who is this Alabama alumnus?

 The Houston Gamblers had a pair of all-USFL kick returners in 1985 who later made trips to the Pro Bowl. One played four years with the Browns and was last seen with the Oilers in 1990; the other did his best work for the Colts (returning five kicks for touchdowns) and finished with the Falcons in 1994. To make this easy, take credit if you can name either one.

 This linebacker probably deserves to be called the best defensive player in the USFL's short history. He was named to virtually every all-league team three years in a row and led the defense of the Philadelphia/Baltimore Stars, the league's best team. He was still doing it in 1996 as the leader of a stout defense that carried a surprising Carolina team to the NFC championship game. Who is this bespectacled fireplug?

 The only man to gain 300 yards passing and 100 yards rushing in the same game did it in 1984 with the L.A. Express and is still playing today. Do you know who he is?

The USFL's all-league tight end in its first season was a 12-year veteran who had caught 364 passes in the NFL with the Raiders and the Colts. He came out of retirement to catch 68 passes for the Oakland Invaders in 1983, then retired again, this time for good. Who is this four-time all-pro?

In his first five years, from 1979 through 1983, this Bengals tight end caught a whopping 257 passes. Jumping to the USFL in 1984, he caught 65 more for the New Orleans Breakers and was an easy choice for the all-league team. He had another 41 receptions in 1985, then returned to Cincinnati that fall. But his return was not a success, and he was finished after spending the 1986 season as a backup with the Packers.

Game 16

3rd Quarter

Nicknames

1. Special Delivery	**5.** Sweetness
2. Speedy	**6.** Tank
3. Spider	**7.** The Throwin' Samoan
4. Stump	**8.** The Toe

9 Too Tall

10 Tuffy

11 Turk

12 Vitamin

13 White Shoes

14 Whizzer

15 Wildcat

Game 16

4th Quarter

Odds and Ends

This tight end caught only 157 passes in a 12-year career, but he played on the first two repeat Super Bowl winners: the Packers and the Dolphins. He also played on the losing side with Miami in Super Bowl VI and was on another NFL champion with Green Bay in 1965 (when there was no Super Bowl). His last game was the Dolphins' 28–26 loss to the Raiders in the 1974 playoffs.

In today's NFL there are two species even rarer than black quarterbacks and head coaches: white cornerbacks and wide receivers. In 1997 the NFL had one white starter at each of these positions, both of them on playoff teams. Who are they?

Conventional wisdom has it that a team without a mobile quarterback will be at the mercy of opponents with a strong pass rush. But in 1988 one of the slowest QBs in the game was sacked only six times while throwing 606 passes. It wasn't a fluke, either; throughout his career he's been one of the hardest for defensive linemen to get their hands on—at least before he throws the ball. Who is this man with the lightning-quick release?

This quintessential power runner hung up his cleats after the 1937 season for a new career as a professional wrestler. With players scarce during wartime, the Bears lured him back in 1943 to play tackle. Trailing in the fourth quarter of the season finale and needing a win to clinch their division title, they took a chance and shifted the old man to fullback. In the last 15 minutes he carried 16 times for 84 yards and a touchdown as the Bears rallied to win. He scored another touchdown in the championship game, a 41–21 victory over the Redskins, and then retired again, permanently this time. Who was this football legend?

Though this Hall of Famer had seen double duty as a center and linebacker earlier in his career, by 1960 he was playing almost exclusively on offense for Philadelphia. But when injuries hit the linebacking corps, our man, now 35, volunteered to go both ways for the rest of the season, which ended with the Eagles winning the championship. Who is this famous iron man?

Joining the Redskins in 1974, this quarterback found himself behind Sonny Jurgensen and Billy Kilmer on the depth chart and threw only 11 passes all season. Not satisfied to stay on the sidelines, he volunteered to return punts when Washington's regular returner was hurt, and actually did a pretty good job of it, averaging 10.5 yards on 15 returns.

Called upon for emergency punting duty or an occasional quick kick at various times throughout his career, this contemporary quarterback has gotten off some real boomers. In

1989, against the Giants, he blasted a 91-yard punt from his own end zone; five years later his only punt of the season was an 80-yarder. Who is this UNLV product whose leg might have been as strong as his arm?

 This Cardinals star started his career as a defensive back but switched to wide receiver in 1981. For much of that season he still served as a nickel back on defense, and in one game he achieved the distinction of making an interception and also catching a touchdown pass—the first time anyone had done that since 1957. After that season he became exclusively an offensive player, and with good reason: he was all-pro in 1983 and '84.

 When his team was short of wide receivers early in the 1996 season, what all-pro defensive back took up the slack and became the first player since 1960 to start the same game on offense and defense? (He didn't do badly, either, catching 36 passes for the season.)

 In the early days of pro football, of course, everybody played offense and defense, but few were as multitalented as this Hall of Famer who led the NFL in passing, punting, and interceptions in 1943. Since this is a pretty well-known feat, even today, I won't tell you what team he played for.

 One of the most versatile players of any era was this Hall of Famer from Virginia, who in 1946 led the NFL in rushing, interceptions, and punt return yardage while playing for the Steelers. Four years earlier he had led in rushing, punt return yardage, and kickoff return average, so this was nothing new for him.

 One of the most interesting multiposition players of the two-platoon era was this punter who spent four years with the Cardinals. In 1968, while averaging 41.6 yards per kick, he

241

also led the NFL in punt return and kickoff return yardage. Who is this Rice alumnus who "went both ways" as a special-teamer?

 This 1995 rookie became something of a sensation when his team used him at quarterback, running back, and wide receiver, often in the same game. He continued to show his versatility in his sophomore season, but by 1997 he had settled in as a starting QB, and a pretty good one at that.

 In an 11-year career with four different teams, this versatile athlete played in five Pro Bowls. He broke in with the Eagles as a defensive back in 1954 and picked off five passes; a year later, playing mainly on offense, he scored touchdowns by rushing and receiving, and returned a kickoff for another score. In 1960, with the Cardinals, he led the NFL in punting and interceptions. He spent his last two seasons with the Packers and finished in 1964 with 35 interceptions and a career average of nearly 44 yards per punt. Who is this former SMU star?

Answers

Game 1

1st Quarter
Milestones
1. Beattie Feathers
2. Gene "Choo-Choo" Roberts
3. Cliff Battles
4. Tom Dempsey
5. Billy Howton
6. Roger Craig
7. Lionel "Little Train" James
8. Lenny Moore
9. Otto Graham
10. Bobby Douglass
11. Fran Tarkenton
12. Randall Cunningham
13. Ron Kramer
14. Ozzie Newsome

2nd Quarter
Second Careers
1. Ed Marinaro
2. Joe Kopcha
3. Bud Grant
4. Merlin Olsen
5. John Brodie
6. Cal Hubbard
7. Hank Soar
8. Bubba Smith
9. Joe Gibbs
10. Deion Sanders
11. Alex Karras
12. Mike Reid
13. Jim Thorpe
14. Fred Williamson

3rd Quarter
Teams
1. Washington Redskins
2. Kansas City Chiefs
3. Chicago Bears
4. Detroit Lions
5. Oakland Raiders; John Madden
6. Baltimore Colts
7. New York Giants
8. Dallas Cowboys; Tom Landry
9. Detroit Lions
10. Pottsville Maroons
11. Robert Irsay bought the Rams and wound up in Baltimore; Carroll Rosenbloom wound up in Los Angeles.
12. The Browns (now Ravens) and 49ers from the AAFC; the Cleveland (later L.A., now St. Louis) Rams from the AFL
13. 1926, when the Frankford Yellow Jackets won the NFL title and the Philadelphia Quakers topped the AFL. Frankford is a neighborhood in Philadelphia.
14. The Boston Redskins, who lost to the Packers 21–6 in the 1936 championship game played in New York. George Preston Marshall took them to Washington in 1937.

4th Quarter
Nicknames
1. Ace Parker, Pug Manders
2. Sam Cunningham, running back of the 1970s Patriots; or running back Byron Morris, with the Steelers and Ravens in the '90s
3. Lance Alworth
4. Gene Lipscomb, defensive tackle with the Rams, Colts, and Steelers
5. Ed "Big Mo", Dick "Little Mo" Modzelewski
6. Hugh Taylor, the Redskins'

leading receiver from 1947 through 1954
7. Norman Esiason
8. Joe Namath
9. Frank Kinard, Brooklyn Dodgers Hall of Fame tackle
10. Walter Andrew Brister III
11. Frank Kilroy, Eagles lineman of the 1940s and '50s

12. Clyde Turner, Hall of Fame center for the Bears in the 1940s
13. Oail Andrews Phillips, Oilers and Saints head coach
14. Jerome Bettis
15. Jim Butler, Falcons running back of the 1970s

Game 2

1st Quarter
AFL Pioneers
1. Clem Daniels
2. Jerry Mays
3. Tom Sestak
4. Chris Burford
5. Jack Kemp, Daryle Lamonica, Buffalo; Babe Parilli, Boston; Dick Wood, New York; George Blanda, Houston
6. Jim Tyrer
7. Art Powell
8. Al Jamison
9. Bob Talamini
10. Ed "Butch" Songin
11. Paul Lowe
12. Larry Grantham
13. Ron Mix
14. Abner Haynes

2nd Quarter
Draft Day
1. Steve Bartkowski
2. Gale Sayers, Dick Butkus
3. Charley Taylor, Paul Krause
4. King Hill
5. Terry Baker
6. Tamarick Vanover
7. Heath Shuler, Gus Frerotte; the Redskins

8. Randy Duncan
9. Don McCauley
10. Eric Swann
11. WR Lynn Swann, 1st round; LB Jack Lambert, 2nd round; WR John Stallworth, 4th round; C Mike Webster, 5th round
12. Jay Berwanger
13. Phil Simms, Steve Fuller, Jack Thompson
14. Steve Emtman

3rd Quarter
All in the Family
1. Qadry and Raghib (Rocket) Ismail
2. Chris and Matt Bahr
3. Sam and Randall Cunningham
4. Clay Matthews Sr., Clay Jr., Bruce Matthews
5. Matt Turk
6. The Nesser brothers; Columbus Panhandles
7. John and Charley Hannah
8. Bob and Brian Griese
9. Browner
10. Jack and Jeff Kemp
11. Bates
12. Steve and Bill Owen
13. Anderson
14. Glenn and Lyle Blackwood

4th Quarter
Moments to Remember
1. Drew Pearson
2. John Riggins
3. Joe Namath, Johnny Unitas
4. Alan Ameche
5. Tommy Brooker
6. Dwight Clark
7. Gary Collins
8. Clarence Davis
9. Ed Podolak
10. Elmer Angsman, Charlie Trippi
11. Vernon Perry
12. Steve Van Buren
13. Tom Tracy
14. Dan Pastorini, Mike Renfro
15. Ricky Watters
16. Pat Summerall

Game 3

1st Quarter
Notorious
1. QB Joe Pisarcik, RB Larry Csonka
2. Billy Cannon
3. Edwin "Alabama" Pitts
4. Jerry Rice
5. John Elway
6. Dave Krieg
7. George "Butch" Atkinson
8. Pittsburgh Steelers
9. Jeff George; Oakland Raiders
10. Terry Bradshaw, Thomas "Hollywood" Henderson
11. John Smith; Miami Dolphins
12. Jack Kemp; Sid Gillman
13. John Riggins
14. Dallas beat Detroit
15. Steve Tasker

2nd Quarter
Teammates
1. Mercury Morris
2. Essex Johnson, Boobie Clark
3. The Steelers' Franco Harris and Rocky Bleier
4. Roland Harper
5. Earnest Byner, Kevin Mack
6. Don Maynard, Art Powell
7. Charley Hennigan, Bill Groman
8. Sonny Randle, Bobby Joe Conrad
9. Bob Hayes, Lance Rentzel
10. John Jefferson, Charlie Joiner
11. Harold Jackson, Stanley Morgan
12. Tony Hill, Drew Pearson
13. Chargers; Jefferson, Joiner, Kellen Winslow
14. Redskins; Gary Clark, Art Monk, Ricky Sanders
15. Charley Taylor, Bobby Mitchell, and tight end Jerry Smith

3rd Quarter
Spring Fever
1. Herschel Walker, Mike Rozier, Doug Flutie
2. Jim Mora
3. Chuck Fusina
4. Kelvin Bryant
5. Anthony Carter, Bobby Hebert
6. Gary Zimmerman
7. Irv Eatman
8. Fred Besana
9. Gary Anderson
10. Frank Minnifield
11. George Allen
12. Stan Talley
13. Sean Landeta

14. Reggie White
15. Craig James

4th Quarter
Point Men
1. Doak Walker
2. Lenny Moore
3. Jim Brown, Gale Sayers
4. O. J. Simpson, Chuck Foreman
5. John Riggins

6. Jerry Rice
7. Emmitt Smith
8. Gordie Soltau
9. Mark Moseley
10. Chip Lohmiller
11. Paul Hornung
12. Jerry Rice
13. Don Hutson
14. Gino Cappelletti
15. Gene Mingo

Game 4

1st Quarter
Yesterday's Heroes
1. William Andrews
2. Mick Tingelhoff
3. Cris Collinsworth
4. Isaac Curtis
5. Timmy Brown
6. Riley Matheson
7. Floyd Little
8. Billy Sims ·
9. Daryle Lamonica
10. Del Shofner
11. Ron Yary
12. Ottis Anderson
13. Tobin Rote
14. Mark Gastineau

2nd Quarter
Men of Letters
1. Dave Meggyesy
2. Jack Tatum
3. Jim Brown
4. Eugene "Mercury" Morris
5. Lee Grosscup
6. Joe Gibbs
7. Jerry Kramer
8. David Kopay, *The David Kopay Story*

9. Doug Williams
10. Conrad Dobler
11. Keyshawn Johnson
12. Lance Rentzel
13. Y. A. Tittle
14. Mike Curtis
15. Charles Haley
16. George Allen
17. Alex Karras
18. Thomas "Hollywood" Henderson

3rd Quarter
Shooting Stars
1. Anthony Johnson
2. Milt Plum
3. James Wilder
4. Howie Ferguson, Packers; Curly Morrison, Browns
5. Bill Kenney
6. Alvin Garrett
7. Adrian Burk
8. Joe Kapp
9. Otis Armstrong
10. R. C. Owens
11. Timmy Smith
12. Bud Schwenk
13. Ted Kwalick
14. Clifton McNeil

4th Quarter
Black Pioneers
1. Art Shell
2. Fritz Pollard
3. Paul Robeson
4. Duke Slater
5. Marlin Briscoe
6. Ray Kemp, Joe Lillard
7. Kenny Washington and Woody Strode
8. Bill Willis, Marion Motley
9. Emlen Tunnell
10. Willie Thrower
11. George Taliaferro
12. Bobby Mitchell
13. Joe Perry, John Henry Johnson, 49ers; Tank Younger, Dan Towler, Rams; and Mo Bassett of the Browns
14. James Harris
15. Doug Williams
16. Joe Gilliam

Game 5

1st Quarter
All in the Family
1. Billy Ray Smith
2. Leo
3. Wonsley
4. Jack and Pug Manders
5. George Wilson, Sr. and Jr.
6. Jeff and Joe Bostic
7. Keith and Jim Fahnhorst
8. Garland and Harold "Red" Grange
9. Brad and Bart Oates
10. Ray and Mike Renfro
11. Ed and Dick Modzelewski
12. Miller and Mel Farr (Mel's sons were Mike and Mel Jr.)
13. Lee Roy and Dewey Selmon
14. Richardson

2nd Quarter
Stand-Ins
1. George Blanda
2. Robert Brooks
3. Frank Reich
4. Don Strock
5. Johnny Clement
6. Max McGee
7. Earl Morrall
8. Bo Molenda
9. Chuck Fenenbock
10. Bobby Scott, Bobby Douglass
11. Sam Baker
12. Jeff Hostetler
13. Wally Lemm
14. Tom Matte
15. Steve Young
16. Rob Carpenter, Gifford Nielsen

3rd Quarter
Milestones
1. Dick Plasman
2. Bill Hewitt
3. Tommy McDonald
4. Ernie Nevers
5. Pete Gogolak
6. Y. A. Tittle
7. Willie "Flipper" Anderson
8. Stephone Paige
9. Jim Benton
10. Anthony Carter
11. Derrick Thomas
12. Norm Willey
13. Spec Sanders
14. Jim Taylor, Jim Nance

4th Quarter
Gridiron Tragedy
1. Darryl Stingley
2. Joe Delaney
3. Reggie Brown
4. Dave Sparks
5. Jeff Alm
6. Ralph Anderson
7. Gene Brito
8. Brian Piccolo
9. Don Fleming
10. Jerome Brown
11. Ernie Davis
12. Mike Utley
13. Dennis Byrd
14. Frank Buncom
15. Don Rogers

Game 6

1st Quarter
Coaching Carousel
1. Jim Lee Howell
2. Vince Lombardi (offense), Tom Landry (defense)
3. Blanton Collier
4. Guy Chamberlin
5. Chuck Noll
6. George Halas (Bears), Curly Lambeau (Packers)
7. Don Shula
8. Les Steckel
9. Buck Shaw
10. Don Coryell
11. Buddy Parker
12. George Wilson
13. Jack Pardee
14. Marty Schottenheimer

2nd Quarter
Notorious
1. Art Schlichter
2. Buddy Ryan and offensive co-ordinator Kevin Gilbride
3. Craig Morton
4. Tony Banks
5. Elmer Layden
6. Dave Hampton
7. Dexter Manley
8. *Heidi*
9. Jim Marshall
10. Dallas Cowboys; Barry Switzer
11. Sammy Baugh
12. Jim Harbaugh; Jim Kelly
13. Ed Meadows
14. Cleveland Browns; Art Modell
15. Al Cowlings

3rd Quarter
Nicknames
1. Gene Roberts, Charlie Justice
2. Carlton Gilchrist
3. Elroy Hirsch
4. David Jones, Rams Hall of Fame defensive end, or Dan Towler, Rams fullback of the 1950s
5. John Riggins
6. Norm Van Brocklin
7. Edgar Manske, end with the Eagles and Bears in the 1930s
8. Roy Lumpkin, a blocking back with Portsmouth and Detroit in the 1930s
9. Wilbur (Pete) Henry, Hall of Fame tackle with the Canton Bulldogs
10. Walt Roberts, wide receiver and kick returner with three teams in the 1960s

11. Willie Anderson, wide receiver with the Rams
12. John Fuqua, Steelers running back of the early 1970s
13. Fred Thurston, Packers guard of the 1960s
14. Harold "Red" Grange
15. Austin Gonsoulin, Denver defensive back of the early 1960s

4th Quarter
Odds and Ends
1. Bruce Smith
2. Steve Spurrier, Tampa Bay; Jim Zorn, Seattle
3. Gale Sayers

4. Jim Plunkett
5. It was shown on both networks simultaneously. A year later it was agreed that they would carry the big game in alternating seasons.
6. The game was televised without announcers
7. John Elway
8. Herschel Walker
9. Preston Pearson
10. Larry Ball
11. Mike Wilson
12. Norm Snead
13. Ben Agajanian

Game 7

1st Quarter
Teams
1. Browns, Colts, Steelers
2. The Cleveland Browns, named (in part) for their great coach, Paul Brown; and the Buffalo Bills, named after "Buffalo Bill" Cody
3. Minneapolis
4. The Bears, who beat the Redskins 73–0 in the 1940 title game
5. The Steelers, with QB Jim Finks
6. New York Giants; Steve Owen
7. Red Hickey
8. Y. A. Tittle was traded to make room for John Brodie; Billy Kilmer and Bobby Waters split time with Brodie in 1961
9. Dallas Cowboys; Tom Landry
10. New England Patriots; Chuck Fairbanks
11. Chicago Bears; Buddy Ryan
12. Miami Dolphins; Bob Matheson

13. Atlanta Falcons; Leeman Bennett
14. New York Giants; Steve Owen; Tom Landry

2nd Quarter
Minor Leagues and Others
1. Don Jonas
2. Los Angeles Bulldogs
3. Coy Bacon
4. Ken Strong
5. Jim Hollingsworth
6. Chuck Mercein
7. Steve Bagarus
8. Tommy Thompson
9. Otis Sistrunk
10. Vince Lombardi
11. Bob Brodhead
12. Ed "Whitey" Michaels
13. Tom Bland
14. Bill Walsh
15. Ed Danowski

3rd Quarter
Get Your Kicks
1. Tommy Davis
2. Yale Lary
3. Jim Bakken
4. Rich Karlis
5. Chris Boniol
6. Jim Fraser, Bob Scarpitto
7. Lou Groza
8. Tony Franklin
9. Reggie Roby
10. Morten Andersen
11. Jerrel Wilson
12. David Ray
13. Steve O'Neal
14. Jim Turner
15. John James

4th Quarter
Breaking In
1. John Gilliam
2. Errict Rhett
3. Bill Paschal
4. Steve Young
5. Sonny Jurgensen
6. Banks McFadden
7. Calvin Hill, father of Grant Hill
8. Eddie Kennison
9. Gaynell Tinsley
10. Pat Coffee
11. Bobby Burnett
12. Bobby Wilson
13. John Brockington
14. Bill Hartman
15. Harlon Hill
16. Paul Robinson
17. Greg Cook

Game 8

1st Quarter
World Football League
1. Paul Warfield, Larry Csonka, Jim Kiick
2. Philadelphia Bell
3. Danny White
4. Pat Haden
5. John Elliott, Gerry Philbin
6. Alfred Jenkins
7. Tim Delaney, Ed Marshall
8. John Gilliam
9. The "action point"
10. Tommy Reamon, J. J. Jennings
11. Charles DeJurnett
12. Keith Krepfle
13. Jack Dolbin, James Scott
14. Steve Foley
15. Ike Harris
16. Gary Danielson
17. Greg Stemrick
18. Anthony Davis

2nd Quarter
Notorious
1. Jimmy Orr, Earl Morrall
2. Jim Hardy
3. Gus Frerotte
4. Chuck Fairbanks
5. Jan Stenerud
6. Garo Yepremian, Mike Bass
7. Randall Cunningham
8. Ken O'Brien
9. Raiders; Ken Stabler, Pete Banaszak, Dave Casper
10. Lawrence Phillips
11. Bo Russell

Answers

12. Bobby Layne
13. Robert Irsay; Baltimore (now Indianapolis) Colts
14. Joe Namath
15. Brian Sipe

3rd Quarter
North of the Border
1. Warren Moon
2. Edgar "Special Delivery" Jones
3. Sam Etcheverry
4. Dick Huffman
5. Doug Flutie
6. Billy Vessels
7. Terry Metcalf
8. Tony Adams
9. Ken Carpenter
10. Cookie Gilchrist
11. Tom Dublinski
12. Mike Nelms
13. DeWitt "Tex" Coulter
14. Glenn Dobbs
15. Martin Ruby

4th Quarter
Time Line
1. 1962; Pete Rozelle
2. 1973
3. 1933
4. 1946; Los Angeles Rams. The 1926 Los Angeles Buccaneers were West Coast in name only and played all games on the road.
5. 1978
6. 1990
7. 1936
8. 1970; Keith Jackson, Howard Cosell, Don Meredith. Frank Gifford replaced Jackson in 1971.
9. 1949
10. 1936
11. Bert Bell; Philadelphia Eagles
12. 1974
13. 1929; the visiting Chicago Cardinals beat the Providence Steam Roller 16–0 on November 6
14. Started in 1986; dropped in 1992 during the off-season (thus it was last used in the 1991 season)
15. The USFL
16. 1943; Lions, Giants

Game 9

1st Quarter
Hall Of Fame
1. Bart Starr
2. Larry Wilson
3. Frank Gifford
4. Bob St. Clair
5. Otto Graham
6. Wayne Millner
7. Alex Wojciechowicz
8. Willie Davis
9. Paul Brown
10. Franco Harris
11. Paul Warfield
12. Bulldog Turner
13. Forrest Gregg
14. Y. A. Tittle, who played for the Colts in 1948 and '49 in the AAFC, and in 1950 in the NFL, after which the team folded
15. Mike Singletary

2nd Quarter
Nicknames
1. Earle Neale, the Eagles' Hall of Fame coach

253

2. Jack Reynolds, linebacker with the Rams and 49ers
3. Fred Williamson, defensive back with the Raiders and Chiefs in the 1960s
4. Thomas Henderson, the Cowboys' controversial linebacker of the late '70s
5. Howard Cassady, Detroit back of the late 1950s
6. Charley Tolar, the Oilers' 5'5", 200-pound fullback of the early 1960s
7. Heartley Anderson, Bears lineman of the 1920s
8. Gerald McNeil, kick returner of the Browns
9. Bengals running back Elbert Woods, creator of the "Ickey Shuffle"
10. Craig Heyward, running back with the Saints and Falcons
11. Hall of Fame running back Joe Perry
12. Earl Girard, back with the Packers and Lions in the 1940s and '50s; or Francis Earp, Packers lineman of the 1920s and '30s
13. O. J. Simpson
14. Elvin Richards, running back for the Giants in the 1930s
15. Lionel James, the Chargers' versatile back of the 1980s

3rd Quarter
Last Hurrahs
1. Sterling Sharpe
2. Cliff Battles

3. Phil Simms
4. Cecil Isbell
5. Sonny Jurgensen
6. Pete Pihos
7. Eddie Brown
8. Don Meredith
9. Don Perkins
10. Kenny Easley
11. Fran Tarkenton
12. Les Bingaman
13. Don Hutson
14. Neil Lomax
15. Dwight Stephenson
16. Davey O'Brien
17. Roger Staubach
18. Ken Riley

4th Quarter
Many Happy Returns
1. Alvin Haymond
2. J. T. Smith
3. Desmond Howard
4. Jack Christiansen
5. Rick Upchurch
6. Eric Metcalf
7. Darrien Gordon
8. Billy "White Shoes" Johnson
9. Travis Williams, Gale Sayers
10. Tyrone Hughes
11. Abe Woodson
12. Billy Thompson
13. Willie Wood
14. Tim Brown
15. Ron Smith
16. Verda "Vitamin" Smith

Game 10

1st Quarter
NFL Pioneers
1. Benny Friedman
2. Jack McBride
3. Mike Michalske
4. Gus Sonnenberg
5. Johnny Blood; his given name was John McNally
6. Jim Thorpe
7. Gus Dorais, Knute Rockne
8. Massillon Tigers
9. Lavern Dilweg
10. Paddy Driscoll
11. Verne Lewellen
12. Clyde Smith
13. Jimmy Conzelman
14. Swede Youngstrom

2nd Quarter
Milestones
1. James Lofton
2. Sammy Baugh
3. Glenn Dobbs
4. Ace Gutowsky
5. Barry Sanders
6. Gale Sayers
7. Tom Fears
8. Johnny Morris
9. Art Monk
10. Lionel Taylor
11. Charley Hennigan
12. Cris Carter; Buddy Ryan
13. Larry Centers
14. Elroy "Crazy Legs" Hirsch

3rd Quarter
Second Careers
1. Bo Jackson
2. Jack Kemp
3. Fred Dryer, star of *Hunter*
4. Glenn Morris
5. Ed "Too Tall" Jones
6. Byron "Whizzer" White
7. K. C. Jones
8. John Havlicek
9. Howie Long
10. Steve Largent
11. Herman Wedemeyer
12. Tom Brown
13. Earle "Greasy" Neale
14. Jim Brown

4th Quarter
Teammates
1. O. J. Simpson
2. Herschel Walker, Joe Morris
3. Jim Brown, Leroy Kelly
4. Leroy Kelly, Larry Brown
5. Emmitt Smith
6. Steve Van Buren
7. Earl Campbell
8. Bob Waterfield, Norm Van Brocklin
9. Paul Christman, Elmer Angsman, and Pat Harder completed the Dream Backfield; Trippi replaced Marshall Goldberg
10. Y. A. Tittle, Joe Perry, Hugh McElhenny, John Henry Johnson
11. Ends Deacon Jones and Lamar Lundy; tackles Merlin Olsen, Rosey Grier, and Roger Brown. Brown replaced Grier in 1967.
12. Ends Carl Eller and Jim Marshall; tackles Alan Page, Gary Larsen, and Doug Sutherland. Sutherland replaced Larsen as a starter in 1974.
13. Ends L. C. Greenwood and

Dwight White; tackles Mean Joe Greene and Ernie Holmes

14. Ends Mark Gastineau and Joe Klecko; tackles Marty Lyons and Abdul Salaam

15. Ends Andy Robustelli and Jim Katcavage; tackles Dick Modzelewski and Rosey Grier. Grier was traded to the Rams and missed the last title game for this group.

Game 11

1st Quarter
Notorious
1. Paul Hornung, Alex Karras
2. Scott Norwood
3. Jackie Smith
4. Hardy Brown
5. Chicago Cardinals
6. Joe Theismann
7. Tim Krumrie
8. Chuck Bednarik
9. Don Chandler
10. Charley Malone
11. Duane Thomas of the Cowboys; interviewer Tom Brookshier
12. Roger Staubach; Phyllis George
13. Otis Sistrunk
14. Earnest Byner
15. Fullback Merle Hapes, quarterback Frank Filchock

2nd Quarter
Yesterday's Heroes
1. Ron Johnson
2. Dwight Clark
3. Tommy Nobis
4. Larry Brown
5. Jim Patton
6. Dick LeBeau, Dave Brown
7. Bob Hayes
8. Charlie Conerly
9. Cedrick Hardman
10. Buddy Dial

11. Bob Hoernschemeyer
12. Jack Youngblood
13. John Brodie
14. Al Wistert

3rd Quarter
North of the Border
1. Frank Tripucka, father of Kelly
2. Dieter Brock
3. Vince Ferragamo
4. Dave Mann
5. Bob Celeri
6. Bob Shaw
7. Joe Theismann
8. Eddie Macon
9. Indian Jack Jacobs
10. Alex Webster
11. Keith Spaith
12. Eddie LeBaron, Gene Brito
13. Mack Herron
14. Pete Liske
15. Bud Grant

4th Quarter
Nicknames
1. Lawrence Taylor
2. Ted Hendricks
3. Charles Edward Greene, great defensive tackle for the Steelers—and no, Joe isn't his real name
4. Eugene Morris, Miami halfback of the early '70s

5. Reggie White
6. Dick Lane, Hall of Fame defensive back
7. Grover Emerson, all-pro guard with Portsmouth and Detroit in the 1930s
8. George Halas
9. Deion Sanders
10. William Perry
11. Kordell Stewart
12. Sammy Baugh
13. Ken Stabler
14. Walt Achui, a back from Hawaii who played with the Dayton Triangles in 1927 and '28
15. Orban Sanders, all-pro back with the New York Yankees in the AAFC

Game 12

1st Quarter
Moments to Remember
1. Keith Lincoln
2. Freeman McNeil
3. Eric Dickerson
4. Lou Groza
5. Ken Houston, Walt Garrison
6. Eagles, Lions; Philadelphia won
7. Sammy Baugh
8. Jack Squirek
9. Chicago Bears; Dave Williams
10. John Taylor
11. Jim O'Brien
12. Mel Renfro, John Mackey
13. John "Frenchy" Fuqua, Jack Tatum
14. A. J. Duhe
15. Redskins, Giants; Washington won
16. John Elway
17. Guard Jerry Kramer, center Ken Bowman; Jethro Pugh

2nd Quarter
All in the Family
1. Tom and Mark Harmon
2. Walt and Lou Michaels
3. Ed "Dutch" Sternaman and his brother Joey
4. Terry and Eric Metcalf
5. Montgomery; Wilbert was the Eagles' ace
6. Michael Dean Perry, William "Refrigerator" Perry
7. Golic
8. Don and David Shula
9. Brian and Bennie Blades
10. Hunt
11. Nelson Munsey, Chuck Muncie
12. Zendejas; Tony was the Oilers' kicker
13. Griffin
14. Ed and Brad Budde

3rd Quarter
Shooting Stars
1. Mark Rypien
2. Jack Hinkle
3. Vinny Testaverde
4. Harry Jagade
5. Warren Wells
6. Clint Longley
7. Steve Owens
8. Don Majkowski
9. Barry Foster
10. Frank Akins
11. Lynn Dickey
12. Cloyce Box

13. Joe Morris
14. Jim Harbaugh

4th Quarter
Men of Letters
1. Jim Kelly
2. Art Donovan
3. Paul Hornung
4. Bernie Parrish
5. Pete Gent
6. John Madden
7. Reggie White

8. Gale Sayers
9. Vince Lombardi
10. George Plimpton
11. Johnny Sample
12. George Ratterman
13. Joe Namath
14. Don Shula
15. Dennis Byrd
16. Larry Csonka, Jim Kiick
17. Alex Hawkins
18. Frank Gifford

Game 13

1st Quarter
Coaching Carousel
1. Joe Gibbs
2. Jock Sutherland
3. Paul Brown
4. Chuck Knox
5. Potsy Clark
6. George Allen
7. Don McCafferty
8. Red Miller
9. Ray Flaherty
10. Weeb Ewbank
11. Hank Stram
12. John McKay
13. Allie Sherman
14. Elmer "Gus" Henderson

2nd Quarter
AFL Pioneers
1. Billy Shaw
2. Fred Arbanas
3. Ben Davidson
4. Paul Maguire
5. Jacky Lee
6. Houston Antwine
7. Dave Grayson

8. Matt Snell
9. Jim Otto
10. Elbert Dubenion
11. Earl Faison
12. Ernie Ladd
13. Hoyle Granger
14. Johnny Robinson

3rd Quarter
Draft Day
1. Everson Walls
2. Joe Jacoby
3. Jim Langer
4. John Huarte
5. Donny Anderson, Jim Grabowski
6. Brian Bosworth
7. Baltimore Colts; Chris Hinton
8. Jim Kelly, Bills; Todd Blackledge, Chiefs; Dan Marino, Dolphins; Ken O'Brien, Jets; Tony Eason, Patriots
9. Cal Rossi
10. Ricky Bell
11. Washington Redskins
12. Steve Walsh
13. Tucker Frederickson

14. Charlie Conerly from Mississippi and Harry Gilmer from Alabama

4th Quarter
Before and After
1. Steve DeBerg
2. Dick Wood
3. David Woodley
4. Bill Austin
5. Curt Knight
6. George Shaw
7. Neal Anderson

8. Mike Livingston
9. Jack Pardee
10. Babe Parilli, Lamar McHan
11. Jan Stenerud, Nick Lowery
12. Bob Waterfield
13. Jeris White
14. Dick Shiner
15. Cliff Stoudt
16. Ray Guy
17. Pete Beathard
18. Scott Hunter

Game 14

1st Quarter
Yesterday's Heroes
1. Chris Hanburger
2. Chuck Howley
3. Dave Wilcox
4. Chuck Foreman
5. Lydell Mitchell
6. Lawrence McCutcheon
7. Ox Emerson, George Christensen
8. Ahmad Rashad
9. Gene Washington
10. Archie Manning
11. Tom Mack
12. Ernest Givins
13. Gary Garrison
14. Claude Humphrey

2nd Quarter
Gridiron Tragedy
1. Gene "Big Daddy" Lipscomb
2. Jim Tyrer
3. Jeff Burkett
4. Stan Mauldin
5. David Overstreet
6. Howard Glenn

7. Al Blozis
8. Mack Lee Hill
9. Chuck Hughes
10. End Bo Farrington, halfback Willie Galimore
11. J. V. Cain
12. Troy Archer
13. Stone Johnson
14. Vic Janowicz
15. Roy Barni

3rd Quarter
Breaking In
1. Johnny Pingel
2. Todd Christensen
3. Dave Parks
4. Tod Goodwin
5. Charley Gogolak
6. Ali Haji-Sheikh
7. Dennis Shaw
8. Leroy Kelly
9. Chris Warren
10. Doug Russell
11. Preston Carpenter
12. Don Looney

13. Reggie Brooks
14. Don Woods
15. George Webster
16. Parker Hall

4th Quarter
Teams
1. Cincinnati Bengals; Sam Wyche
2. Buffalo Bills; Marv Levy
3. Providence Steam Roller, 1928
4. Dallas Texans, in 1952
5. Chicago Bears, in 1985
6. Chicago Bears, who lost to the

Giants in 1934 and Redskins in 1942
7. Washington Redskins; George Allen
8. Denver Broncos
9. Detroit Lions; Jack Christiansen, Yale Lary
10. Chicago Cardinals
11. Cleveland Browns
12. Baltimore Colts
13. Redskins. The song, of course, is "Hail to the Redskins."
14. Detroit Lions

Game 15

1st Quarter
Minor Leagues and Others
1. Claude Watts
2. Mel Reid
3. Jackie Robinson
4. Ozzie Simmons
5. Jeff Van Note
6. Bob and Rudy Kuechenberg
7. Tod Goodwin, Jack Ferrante
8. Sid Gillman
9. Jim "King" Corcoran
10. Bob Tucker
11. Tom Harmon, Michigan; John Kimbrough, Texas A&M
12. Ken Stabler
13. Garo Yepremian
14. Elliott Ormsbee
15. Tom Kennedy

2nd Quarter
Teammates
1. Mal Kutner, Bill Dewell
2. Mac Speedie, Dante Lavelli
3. The Electric Company; guards

Reggie McKenzie and Joe DeLamielleure
4. Tackles Joe Jacoby and George Starke, guards Russ Grimm and Mark May, and center Jeff Bostic
5. Mark Duper, Mark Clayton
6. Vance Johnson, Mark Jackson, Ricky Nattiel
7. Art Monk, Gary Clark, Ricky Sanders
8. Doug Betters, Bob Baumhower, Kim Bokamper, Bob Brudzinski, and the Blackwood brothers, Lyle and Glenn
9. Dick Anderson, Jake Scott
10. Cliff Harris, Charlie Waters
11. Dan Towler, Dick Hoerner (who left in 1952), Tank Younger
12. Rickey Jackson, Vaughan Johnson, Sam Mills, Pat Swilling. Jackson and Swilling both recorded more than 100 sacks; Swilling was the 1991 Defensive Player of the Year.
13. Jack Ham, Jack Lambert, Andy Russell

14. Ron Jaworski and Randall Cunningham
15. Eddie LeBaron, Don Meredith

14. Thurman Thomas; Buffalo Bills
15. Bears QB Jim McMahon; Packers lineman Charles Martin

3rd Quarter
Notorious
1. Sid Luckman
2. Frank Tripucka
3. Al Dorow
4. George Blanda
5. George Blanda again
6. Jim Hart
7. John Hadl
8. Fran Tarkenton
9. Ken Stabler
10. Richard Todd
11. Vinny Testaverde
12. Leon Lett
13. Y. A. Tittle

4th Quarter
Milestones
1. Eric Dickerson
2. Sid Luckman
3. Y. A. Tittle
4. Paul Krause
5. Dick "Night Train" Lane
6. Lester Hayes
7. Don Doll
8. Steve Van Buren
9. Joe Perry
10. Frank Filchock
11. Ken Anderson
12. Johnny Unitas
13. Joe Namath
14. Dan Marino

Game 16

1st Quarter
All in the Family
1. Bill and Joe Osmanski
2. Merlin and Phil Olsen
3. Tice
4. Keith and Kerry Cash
5. George Sauer, Sr. and Jr.
6. Don and Joe Don Looney
7. Saul
8. Jay and Joel Hilgenberg
9. Brock
10. Garrard (Buster) Ramsey, his brother Knox, and defensive back Ray
11. Rooney
12. Gene and Marvin Upshaw
13. Sterling and Shannon Sharpe
14. Dub Jones and his son Bert

2nd Quarter
Spring Fever
1. Mel Gray
2. Kent Hull
3. Head coach Jack Pardee, offensive coordinator Mouse Davis, and quarterback Jim Kelly
4. Johnnie Walton
5. William Fuller
6. Joe Cribbs
7. Richard Johnson
8. Herschel Walker
9. Buddy Aydelette
10. Gerald McNeil, Clarence Verdin
11. Sam Mills
12. Steve Young
13. Raymond Chester
14. Dan Ross

3rd Quarter
Nicknames

1. Edgar Jones, halfback with the Browns in the AAFC
2. Leslie Duncan, defensive back and league-leading kick returner with the Chargers in the 1960s and Redskins in the '70s
3. Carl Lockhart, Giants defensive back from 1965 through 1975
4. Cardinals running back Lyvonia Mitchell
5. Walter Payton
6. Paul Younger, Rams fullback in the 1950s
7. Jack Thompson, quarterback with the Bengals and Buccaneers in the early 1980s
8. Lou Groza
9. Cowboys defensive end Ed Jones
10. Alphonse Leemans, Hall of Fame back with the Giants
11. Glen Edwards, the Redskins' Hall of Fame tackle
12. Verda Smith, the Rams' star kick returner circa 1950
13. Billy Johnson, punt returner and receiver with the Oilers and Falcons
14. Byron White, rushing leader in 1938 and '40
15. George Wilson, all-pro tailback who led Providence to the 1928 championship

4th Quarter
Odds and Ends

1. Marv Fleming
2. Jason Sehorn, Giants cornerback; Ed McCaffery, Broncos wide receiver
3. Dan Marino
4. Bronko Nagurski
5. Chuck Bednarik
6. Joe Theismann
7. Randall Cunningham
8. Roy Green
9. Deion Sanders
10. Sammy Baugh
11. Bill Dudley
12. Chuck Latourette
13. Kordell Stewart
14. Jerry Norton